OUT ON A LEASH

Also by Shirley MacLaine

SHIRLEY MacLAINE

OUT ON A LEASH

Exploring the Nature of Reality and Love

ATRIA BOOKS

New York   London   Toronto   Sydney   Singapore

ATRIA BOOKS
1230 Avenue of the Americas
New York, NY 10020

Copyright © 2003 by Shirley MacLaine

Photographs on insert pages 1, 3, 4, 5, 6, 8 (bottom), 10 (bottom),
11 (top), 14–5, and 16 are courtesy of David Weininger; photographs in the insert on pages 2 (bottom), 7, 8 (top), 9, 10 (top),
11 (bottom), 12–13 are courtesy of the author; photograph in
the insert on page 2 (top) is courtesy of Roger Wood/Corbis.

Design by Joel Avirom, Jason Snyder, and Meghan Day Healey

ISBN: 0-7434-8506-8

First Atria Books hardcover edition October 2003

10 9 8 7 6 5 4 3 2 1

ATRIA BOOKS is a trademark of Simon & Schuster, Inc.

Manufactured in the United States of America

For information regarding special discounts for bulk purchases,
please contact Simon & Schuster Special Sales at 1-800-456-6798
or business@simonandschuster.com

For Allene, who put wind under Terry's wings,
For Mort, who always understood me,
And for Terry, who helps me live in the light
of expressing what we both feel.

"All knowledge, the totality of all questions and answers, is contained in the dog."

—*Franz Kafka*

"I explained to St. Peter I'd rather stay here,

Outside the Pearly Gate.

I won't be a nuisance, I won't even bark,

I'll be very patient and wait.

I'll be here, chewing on a celestial bone,

No matter how long you may be.

I'd miss you so much if I went in alone,

It wouldn't be Heaven for me."

—*Author Unknown*

Introduction

When our children grow up and leave home to raise families of their own, and the past becomes a memory of things we are no more, we are faced with inventing a new future. This is the moment when we are finally free to make choices outside the powerful tug of expectation, ambition, and struggle. We have reached what I call the age of reason. Now we can choose to live not for others, but for ourselves, and we can take time to explore a life of inner knowledge for which we were always too busy.

For me the chaos of city life, heightened by the fear of terrorism and the culture of technology that forced me to remember codes and numbers to access even my own personal information, further pushed me to reevaluate what life should be about. I realized I was inundated by information and misinformation from our leadership and the media—and that it was slowly eroding my spirit. I was falling out of touch with my own inner truth. These realizations were slow in coming, but the important thing is that they finally did arrive.

So several years ago I decided to make my year-round home on an 8,000-acre Spanish land grant that used to be an old cattle ranch just outside of Santa Fe, New Mexico. It's a peaceful place, and sometimes deafeningly silent, with ancient energies that communicate to me in nameless ways. I live there with people who take care of me, and friends who come and stay, as well as nine dogs, three horses, ducks, platoons of birds, a pond, streams, deer, elk, bears, mountain lions, coyotes, and a host of spectacular plant life. But the most important being on the ranch is my little dog, Terry.

I "acquired" Terry in Malibu, California, where I lived for fifty years and still keep a place for meetings. She and I grew closer and closer during the few years it took me to distance myself from Malibu, with its easy access to the movie business, and to shift my life to the high desert wilderness. But as with all events that are life-changing, I woke up one morning and knew in my soul that the city part of my life was over. I was moving on to a new adventure that would lead me to realize that perhaps Terry had acquired *me*.

This book is about hearing a deeper song of being that has made me more optimistic about what the future of life on this planet could be. It is based on the truth as I see it, and as it has been shown to me through the eyes of a dog. More to the point, I'm having a new experience with love. I have deeply enjoyed the love of children, friends, lovers, a husband, work, creativity, fame, travel, success, money, politics, controversy, and even struggle. But the love that has come to me through Terry is an exultant confirmation that love exists in many realities and forms, all of them longing to be acknowledged through wisdom, humor, simplicity, silence, and the wordless language of the heart.

Here is an account of what Terry is teaching me, now that I am taking time to listen. Her thoughts as they come to me are not articulated in English, but in a purer, more direct form, in a language I call "humanimal." I know that I am touching deeper truths because of the knowledge Terry shares with me, so I've set down those insights into words here, in hopes that you may benefit from them as well.

This book, then, is a rumination, a conversation between Terry and me. Those of you who have an animal and live in close proximity to nature will understand immediately. If you haven't allowed an animal or nature to "acquire" you, the journey through yourself will take a little longer. Either way, this journey is the only one worth taking.

The answers we seek are ours to create.

Shirley

Have I discovered that I am capable of unconditional love? Sometimes I lie in bed, holding Terry, overcome with the wonder of it all. She has slowed me down, letting me understand that time is just an invention of man as she takes me to a world where everything is known concurrently. Her tolerance gives me peace. Her free spirit gives me courage. Her playfulness entertains me beyond all comedy I've ever known. Terry negotiates my life as though she has traveled it before, and she knows my thoughts as though she were part of me. We communicate in a game that is sometimes playful and at other times profoundly serious, because we both realize it is the basis for my newfound ability to feel and accept love without reservation.

I have had many female friends whom I enjoyed because they understood the power of allowing others just to be, the power of patience, and even the power of subservience at certain times. But I've never had a girlfriend like this. She is my confidante, my sense of home, and my deepest venture into the intimacy of myself. She has taken me on a road away from this world into a new world of happiness and inner peace. The happiness comes from what I've found; the inner peace comes from what I did not even know was there before.

I lie with Terry and understand for the first time what it means to weep for the sheer joy of it. Her purity humbles me. Her warmth brings me comfort, and her breathing is a reminder that God has created involuntary acts so that we need not always control and manipulate our surroundings to survive; simply by being we can also evolve.

When Terry stirs in her sleep, it always makes me smile. When I hear her moving through her dreams I long to join her there, and I wonder if she can remember her dreams in the morning. I wish I could understand the dimensions of her life that she seems so fully able to appreciate in mine. She always seems to be telling me something, something that I haven't yet touched, or something that I am unwilling to embrace in the world I understand.

When I'm away from Terry I'm back to square one. I want to return home, where I know she waits to give me the secrets of the night, to share her knowledge of the moon. She waits for me to understand what it is to be female. She wants me home from the yang world, and I know the wait is sometimes too long. I wonder where she is. Is she sitting by the front door? Lying on the bed with her feet up in the air? Is she feeling alone? Why *did* I leave her to come out into a world that is so confused, so upset, and so off balance when I can be with Terry in a state of bliss, where another living being accepts me totally and I accept her the same way?

Terry weaves her bouncing spirit through the threads of my life. I hug her with my heart. She *is* my heart and part of my soul, playing through the shadows of all my concerns and lighting them up with her bubbly prancing. Why have I never felt this way before? I am at once exalted and ashamed because I have known so many, have given myself to and taken from so many, and yet this is the first time that I feel peace. My old world sometimes wonders where I've gone. What am I doing? Who am I with? Why have I disappeared? Why do I not seem to mind that I have disappeared?

I feel removed from all but my closest friends. As for the rest, I find I have nothing to contribute to their competitive conversations. I am not particularly interested in their moneymaking prowess, in their overachieving, and their living by the rules. I am even beginning to be bored by their favorite topic: aging. I am not much interested in gyms and workouts, or even vanity, anymore; my face is becoming prettier to me as I learn to love myself. What I *am* interested in is taking a walk for the sheer pleasure of every step. I'm interested in eating much smaller amounts of food and exercising moderately, because I feel better when I do. I'm interested in caring for my skin and my face because it loves attention. And yes, I am interested in loving the space in which I live and the person that I am in this space. Here Terry loves me and accepts me, sometimes with hints of sadness for what I don't understand, and with steady joy for what I might someday come to know.

Terry

*My Mistress Mother can be **so** serious sometimes. She thinks too much. She asks too many questions. My canine mother let me join my MM so I could teach her that she already knows much more than she thinks she does.*

*On the bright side, my Mistress Mother does call me Twinklebutt, Sparklefeet, and Honeyhunk. And she **can** just let herself have a good time with me, even if she wants to know **why**. I try to tell her that when she's happy, that's all that matters.*

I have a wonderful time with my MM. She hardly ever scolds me. When she does it's usually because I have decided to provoke her. I like to stir her up, and besides, she can be really cute when she's upset. She does feel guilty about it afterward, which I love to put to good purpose—

along with all the other emotions that a child can bring out in a mother.

My MM truly does care for me. She feeds me whatever I want, which is why my Twinklebutt sometimes won't fit under an airplane seat. She also takes me almost everywhere. She drives me in the car, which I love. I chase my shadows in the car. I chase shadows anywhere, which really intrigues MM because she doesn't really understand what a shadow is. I will have to teach her.

When I'm in the car, I love to hurl myself against the windows, barking and snarling. None of this has anything to do with my real feelings, but it entertains my MM and it tests her ability to focus when she's on the road. I notice that she's very careful to take my leash off when I'm in the car, so I don't accidentally hang myself. I know we never die, so that wouldn't be a problem for me, but she carefully avoids anything that could be dangerous to me.

I have known my Mistress Mother before, in an Egyptian lifetime, when I was the animal god Anubis, and she was a minor, mortal princess. As a deity who had knowl-

edge of the afterlife in ancient Egypt, I presided on a throne decorated with animals and hieroglyphs, and my MM sat at my feet inquiring incessantly about the nature of life and what happened after we died. I tried to teach her then, but she never really understood, so I'm going to try to teach her again in this lifetime. (In those days all Egyptians were grappling with the same questions, although I must say they were further along in their understanding than people are today; now people are too cynical and suspicious.)

I have told MM that I'm going to live eighteen years in human time. That's a good number because eight and one is nine. I don't know if she knows that's the number of completion, but I do. She's going to live much longer than that, and one of the reasons she will is because I am going to bring her the gift of simplicity. That is why I am in her life: to cut down on everything but the simple joy of being happy.

I watched my MM for a long time before I decided to be born, then I began this part of my journey with MM in a pet shop in Malibu. I don't really remember how I got into the pet shop, but she was walking by on her way to do some shopping. I could see that one of the big questions in her lit-

tle human mind was: what is love? I felt that it was time for

her to buy me, so I called her in. "Come into the pet shop.

Come into the pet shop." When she walked in I began my

little sparkle-footed, twinkle-butted dance around the cage.

I knew that she had been a dancer, so I put on my best

prancing steps and they definitely got her attention.

My Mistress Mother likes to think she is practical.

When she learned that I was a rat terrier she thought I

could help with mice on the ranch where she lives. Con-

cerned that the other dogs on the ranch might kill a cat, my

MM had been looking for another ranch dog, which was

good. She was ready to hear me want her, call her, and

demand to be owned and brought up by her.

My Mistress Mother doesn't do much of anything

that doesn't have practical use. Some think she is a good

actor. Others think she is a good dancer, or singer. For my

MM, none of these measure up to her sense of being a

practical person. I have watched her choose to play the-

aters that are closer to the freeway turnoff instead of the-

aters that have good acoustics or even a great stage. No, she would rather be practical.

My MM did, after all, have a Canadian mother, and Canadian people tend to be practical. Her father, on the other hand, was a dreamer, although sometimes the dream was no fun. He grew up in a small town in Virginia, and looking down on him I saw that he used to tie dogs' and cats' tails together and watch them fight (which may be why my MM has this fascination with inner peace). Also, she was born at the end of April, which makes her a Taurus, an earth sign, so she likes having her feet planted solidly on the ground. Some would say her head is now too much in the stars, but she even looks at the starry aspect of things in a very practical way. Although she seems to be one of the free spirits of the planet, she never really has thrown caution to the winds. She has always had a way of making sure her survival was ensured. She thinks that is her job in life. I know that mine is to help her get over that. Not that I don't want her to survive, but I understand that she should have more sparkle-footed, twinkle-butted moments.

Shirley

Terry is part of my destiny. She drew me into her life because it was time. In fact she imposed herself on what I thought was my well-regulated time. She insisted on giving love to me, on being so adorable that I had to welcome her into my life. Terry has given me a new vista, full of flowers, bees, birds, and worms. She has brought new kinds of play to me. She has given the chase new meaning. She makes frolicking with insects an alert game. She even gives begging dignity. She begs for play, food, touch; she begs for my arms, my lap, my warmth, at times my love itself. And all the while she is teaching me by example.

Terry lives in profound honesty. She lunges and grabs at life with barks and snorts and kisses and jumps. She asks for love unashamedly and returns it without

15

reservation. She is my teacher, my friend, my sister, my daughter, and my mother. She is now part of me. I cannot leave her alone for more than a few hours. I know that she is self-sufficient in her own soul, but I also know how much she enjoys being with me. When I'm away, does she wonder whatever happened to me? I think so, because I feel the same way.

Time doesn't matter anymore, except to remind me to come home to her. How is it possible that Terry now rules my schedule? How is it possible that through the merging of our souls she now dictates where I live? How is it possible that I am no longer free, yet I know that I have found true freedom? I no longer travel unless Terry will be happy with it. I won't stay out all night with friends because I know that the other half of me is waiting. I'm much more meticulous with my habits because I have to be careful about hers: I have water with me at all times because I know Terry needs water at all times; I brush my hair more frequently because I like to brush *her* hair more frequently.

How is it possible that another little soul could have so imposed herself on my life that I have changed the very fundamentals by which I live? She has made me read differently, think differently, and act differently. I feel that I am loved without judgment, without boundaries, and without blame. In response to Terry I am loving unconditionally for the first time.

I think I may have known Terry throughout the ages. She may even be here to teach me that I can satisfy my incessant search for truth and meaning before I die. Perhaps she is a messenger from God. Perhaps in her warm little body and soul lies all I need to know of life and death and spirit. Perhaps it is all a joke that the universe is playing on me. The truth is hiding in plain sight. Perhaps the TRUTH is my dog Terry, and the joke is that dog spelled backward is God.

Terry

My MM keeps asking herself, What is love? From what I can see, most humans don't know the answer to that question. They don't know how to love, or do it for the wrong reasons, and what starts out being about what they think is love and romance usually ends up being about money. My MM's questions about love are the reason I'm in her life. Interestingly, male canines and male humans don't have much to say on this subject that's helpful. It's the female of the species that seems to be most profoundly interested.

I deeply love my MM and she deeply loves me too, but she doesn't know how to deal with it. Every now and then, to snap her out of confusion, I will spring myself up into her arms, drag her shoes around and use them for chewy toys, or stare at the Milk-Bone box, all to distract her. My favorite trick, though, is to refuse to get out of the car in the middle of a snowy winter. I will sit in the car, shivering in the cold, just so she will worry about me instead of her own problems. Sometimes, if she wants to go for a beach walk in the warm sun, I will wait until the sun goes down before I'll say, "Okay, now I'm ready." This doesn't seem to really bother her, but it does bring her back to thinking that I am a God posing as a dog.

Sometimes I like to play princess. (I wouldn't dare play a god in this lifetime.) My MM has arranged with a half-dozen restaurants in various cities to allow me to sit beside her in a booth when she's having a delicious seven-course meal. Whether I'm in a restaurant in Santa Fe or a hotel in New York, people might say, "Oh, here comes Princess Terry again." I sit there exactly like royalty and refuse any meat bones that the cook might whip up for me in the kitchen so they'll know that's beneath my dignity. They all think it's charming; I know it's absurd, because I prefer people food.

It is often said that dogs have masters and cats have staff. I am a dog that has a staff. Of course, even a princess like me has to be careful not to be too aloof, so I insist on greeting every human I see, regardless of who he or she may be; an upright statesman or a beggar lying on the street both get the same greeting. I jump on them and kiss their faces. Most of the time I lightly nip their noses too, and whenever I do that they always say, "Animals love me, especially dogs."

Whenever I want people to pay more attention to me, I assume a dignified seated position and then I shiver. Then they all come over to me, sometimes as many as a dozen people at once, and say, "Oh, the poor little thing, why is she shivering?" They give me a treat or they pet me, or they chastise my MM. "Why is she so afraid?" Of course I am neither cold nor afraid. I'm ready to start teaching my next lesson.

I also love to twirl for people. I twirl around two or three times and they think I'm so talented. Then they give me treats and fuss over me. I don't remember how I learned to twirl. It might have been from watching MM dance. Whenever we have company I twirl.

My Mistress Mother once took me to a very fancy party where several elderly women, covered with expensive glittering stones, thought it was shocking that a dog should be in attendance, roaming between legs and feet under the table. I heard my mistress say, "Well, just wait, soon you'll be feeding her off your plate." And, sure enough, before long I was being fed from a half-dozen laps. I twirled many times that night.

I enjoy being adorable, but it's difficult with the harem of dogs at my mistress's ranch, because the females are on to me. However, I control every new environment I'm in, within about, I would say, three minutes; one for mind, one for body, and one for spirit.

My favorite environment is my MM's bed, where I love to sleep curled up in her arms. I also enjoy pushing her out of bed with my legs, which are very strong because she takes me on long walks. In Malibu we walk on the beach, and on the ranch we walk in the mountains. I also like to put my head up above the covers so that I can snuggle against my MM's cheek. She loves cuddling me. She buries her face in my fur and squiggles around with her nose. She loves the way I smell because she puts parsley in my water to prevent the doggie smell that most humans don't like. I smell very sweet. I've heard a lot of MM's friends say that.

I like to protect my MM, and sometimes I even protect her in her sleep. I can enter my Mistress Mother's dreams, so if she is dreaming about something scary, I sit on her stomach and bark to wake her up.

Without a wake-up bark, my Mistress Mother is a late riser. She likes to go to bed around two in the morning and get up about ten, so now I've made that natural for me. When the clock squeals for no good reason, an appointment or something, I ignore it. I crawl farther under the covers, exactly where my MM would like to be if she wasn't so anxious to do what is expected of her.

When MM begins her morning exercises that's when I like to sneak out, jump on her back and nip at her hair, or lick the nape of her neck—anything to turn her away from the boring drone of that CNN. Then I will go grab a toy. I know where I've hidden everything in every single room; I have toys under every single pillow or table. I rotate my toys, finding the ones most difficult for my MM to locate. I will then jump in the air and throw the toys, knowing MM will turn away from the news to catch them.

I never understood why it's so important to know what's going on in the world every single day, especially when most of it isn't exactly true anyway. But then I suppose my MM has no idea why I stop dozens of times every fifty yards when we walk. No matter how many mornings we walk the same path, God gives me more to see, and smell, and understand. I love it when my MM notices some small thing in my world, freeing her from hers, even if only for a breath. I take enormous pleasure in making her stop many times, knowing this keeps her from being so goal-oriented.

When my Mistress Mother wants to take me out in the snow or the cold, I'm perfectly happy to go, but sometimes I don't want to wear the coats she buys for me, which include a beautiful yellow wool coat, a plaid coat, and even a raincoat. But if I just want to go out in my own natural coat instead, I simply crawl under the middle of our big bed where she can't get me dressed. She always waits for me and usually when I come out she doesn't force me to wear anything.

I hope you don't think that I'm poking fun at my Mistress Mother's love for me. That's not it at all. What I am really doing is trying to teach her to be simpler in the ways of joy, simpler in the ways of love, simpler in the ways of life. One of the best ways to do that is through humor.

Did you hear about the dyslexic agnostic who lies awake at night wondering if there really is a Dog?

Shirley

I love to walk. I've done so much rigorous exercise in order to stay in shape for dancing that I'm happy to take it slower in my advancing years. LSD walking, I call it: Long, Slow, Distance walking. I'm learning to allow the path to become the journey. In this way I'm not only savoring the exquisite beauty of nature but also the pleasures of ruminating, of sifting and sorting through my own thoughts and feelings.

With Terry accompanying me I'm learning there are many dimensions to being alive that I never considered before, simply because I always felt it necessary to have a purpose. When I walked across northern Spain (the Santiago de Compostela Camino) I realized how much of an overachiever I was. I'm learning how to let that go, and walking, especially with Terry, has helped me do so. Walking has become a form of meditation. I can't say I've attained the ability to walk without having a single thought, but I am enjoying the new experience of just *being*. I'm learning that from Terry.

I would like to be able to happily walk without knowing where I'm going. I would like to be able to walk farther than is safe. I would like to walk away, to let myself off my own leash to be in a place where my thoughts and feelings can exist solely for their own sakes. Terry can do that already. She has a sense of peace that I aspire to. There's nothing like a dog to help you know who you are—and what you're capable of being.

When Terry and I are in Malibu one of our favorite pleasures is taking a long walk on the beach. I'm no longer surprised when Terry begins to jump with excitement as soon as I just *think* about going to the beach. Often she seems to know my thoughts before I do. By the time I've put on my sun hat Terry is down the stairs and out on the sand. For the next few minutes she leaps and barks until I throw something she can chase. When my sense of balance is challenged I negotiate a little moon-walk to avoid stepping on Terry dancing underfoot, which excites her even more.

Terry's favorite beach activity is chasing wet sand, so I pick up a long-handled scoop that I'll use to fling the sand as far out in front of me as I can. Terry will then run like a streak of furry lightning, her paws barely touching the ground, to launch herself twisting and twirling on the ocean breeze to catch every possible grain of sand. I don't need to stock up on Frisbees, or rubber balls, or anything else a pet store has to offer. Wet sand is all she wants. When we pass other beach walkers, they stare in disbelief at what Terry does in the air, and at the rudimentary nature of her chasing toy. She likes the sand because all the other dogs like balls and sticks. I don't mind; not only do I get a good upper body workout this way, I also never have to bend over to retrieve anything. Terry would never lower herself to bring an object back to lie at my feet any-way. Such an act would be demeaning.

Terry stops unexpectedly, still as a perched statue on the beach in front of me, and waits for me to catch up. This gives me the opportunity to step into a fast-paced stride. I reach Terry and keep right on going. She, meantime, maintains her frozen stance, which finally forces me to turn back to get her. She loves interrupting my stride.

When another dog approaches, Terry simply sets her ears in antenna position and waits. If the new dog seems friendly, Terry's tail wags like a runaway metronome and she romps to meet her new friend. If the dog looks hostile, Terry waits for the dog to reach her, then rolls over on her back and flattens her ears in supplication, allowing the dog to have his way with her. This is actually a form of seduction. Today she allowed a big German shepherd to believe he was in control, and then she bounded to her feet and began to play. The huge male was astonished and thrown off balance. Sometimes she keeps playing until the game becomes a romp, but today she simply trotted off, leaving the huge shepherd abandoned and confused, a helpless giant.

Terry

I love to play on the beach with my MM. Sometimes when I'm chasing sand I will see huge dogs come bounding toward me. I always roll over on my back and let them think they are in charge. But I have this act down. MM knows it too. She's never concerned for me because she knows that in the end TERRY RULES.

It's people in uniforms who sometimes bother me. Once the Dog Police came out on the beach to arrest me and take me to dog jail because I didn't have my leash on. I knew what they were thinking so I jumped into my MM's arms and started my shivering act. MM was furious; she held me close and screamed at them. She called them Fascists and threatened to sue them if they hurt me. They were very upset by her behavior and turned away, leaving me safe. I licked my MM's face and understood more than ever how much she loves me. She knows that as we walk through this lifetime together I am her spiritual teacher. She is out on my leash . . . my spiritual leash.

I love to walk on the beach when the sun goes into the water. Sometimes this means the moon will go up soon. If it goes up tonight maybe I can use it to teach MM more about the light of reflection. After all, everything is a reflection. Although I'm happy here in Malibu I can't wait to go to our ranch in New Mexico because there are other kinds of reflections there: reflections of trees and birds and insects and shadows from the rocky mountains and hills, and of course reflections from my family of dog friends. And there are no humans in uniforms.

Shirley

As we romp and play at the water's edge, I am in turmoil. I'm being offered a role in a movie being shot partly on location in Northern Ireland. It's a wonderful script with Lord Richard Attenborough directing, but I haven't been able to find a way to bring Terry with me, and the location shoot will take six weeks. The U.K. has a quarantine requirement for dogs. The old 180-day quarantine has been lifted, but I don't understand what the new procedures are. Even if Terry would have to remain in quarantine for only a few weeks, I don't think I could bear it. The thought of her in a cage for just one night breaks my heart.

I've contacted the British embassy, the airlines, and veterinarians, but nobody will give me a straight answer when I ask if there's a way to get around the quarantine. It's far-fetched, but I've been thinking of hiring someone to fly with Terry to Germany or France and then drive her into the U.K. I would want to be with her, though, for the drive, which would mean adding a week of extra time to my schedule.

When Elizabeth Taylor shot a movie in the U.K., she rented a yacht where she could work and live with her dog. I can't afford a yacht. Believe me, I know all this is completely impractical, if not delusional. Will I really allow my dog to be the determining factor in my career? I have good friends who would give Terry the best of care, but I'd still worry so much about her being alone— not to mention how *I'd* feel being without her.

Terry senses my thoughts as she runs toward me and leaps into my arms. I look down at her as she gazes into my face unflinchingly, the rolling waves reflected in her eyes. She kisses my hand and nips my fingers. If I were away from her, would I feel her giving me lick-kisses on my cheek or pushing against my legs, only to look down and find that she wasn't really there?

Terry

Poor MM. She is plagued with worries, like a ringing in her ears that won't go away. I am everything to her, but she doesn't trust that I am also everywhere. I could put my spirit on a wave and send it across the ocean to her, but I don't want her to know that yet. It's time for her to decide what love means. I know she'll be so unhappy without me, there's no way she could focus on her work: She'll wonder, maybe Terry's not getting her vitamins, maybe Terry's not eating, or maybe Terry's sulking under the bed.

I don't like it when my MM has to be away from me, and I know it's not particularly sensitive, but sometimes when she comes home I find ways to communicate my displeasure so she'll think twice before leaving me next time. I'll turn away if she strokes me. I'll sleep with my *back to her if she takes a nap. Basically, I'll have nothing to do with her until I decide she has gotten my point. I know this hurts her but I **really** don't like her to be away. Once, to show my displeasure, I pooped on her white rug even though she left the outside door open for me. That really made her upset, which upset me, and neither of us should be upset.*

Once my MM left me for two whole days. She had some important business and couldn't take me with her. Her housekeeper, Nellie, was cleaning on the other side of the house, and I was under our big bed pouting and feeling miserable, so I decided to tell Nellie how I felt. Using my soul language, I shouted very loud, "Tell her NO. I mean it! NO!"

Nellie was really scared because she thought someone else was in the house. She came running to our bedroom and looked around. I yelled again, "Tell her not to go away for so long again!"

Nellie ran away, terrified.

When my MM came back, Nellie told her what had happened. She said she had heard a ghost. But MM knew it was me—and she has never left me for that long since. That's the truth!

And that's what I'll do if she can't take me to Northern Ireland. I'll make the "NO" so loud she'll hear me across the ocean. The producer of the movie is still having trouble raising all the money anyway, so I don't have to worry for a while.

However, when my Mistress Mother does go out for a few hours without me, I do appreciate it when she tells me what she wants me to do when she's gone, like to take care of the house, or to make sure everything is peaceful. This way I know I have a job to do. I usually try to stay in communication with her when she's driving on the road because, as I've said before, I love to go in the car with her. I always know when she's coming home and I always go right by the door when she's about a mile away so she'll think I've been sitting there the whole time.

SHIRLEY MACLAINE

Shirley

I think I understand Terry's inner life—her sorrows and her joys—but she is still a dog and something about her will always remain a little elusive. Terry may not be able to study physics, or paint a picture, but I bet she could find her way across the country to come back to me. What is intelligence? Terry is capable of remarkable tranquillity, and according to Hindu philosophers tranquillity is the highest emotion because it lies underneath all the others, waiting to be discovered. Terry is teaching me to feel more purely and more intensely, and not to be so wracked by intellectual and emotional ambivalence. I've always thought of myself as direct and honest, but I am nothing along those lines compared to Terry.

Our human language is full of indications of how

much dogs mean to us. Someone who is a champion is "top dog." Somebody who is not favored to win is an "underdog." People compete in a "dog-eat-dog" world, and suffer through the "dog days" of August. When our priorities are misplaced, the "tail wags the dog." A book that's well worn is "dog-eared." People who look victimized have "hangdog" expressions. Why do we sometimes call people a "dirty dog"? And why is a "bitch" the most humiliating thing you can call a woman? Dogs have not only stepped into our hearts but into our lexicons.

If dogs are important to us, there is ample evidence that the depth of feeling runs both ways. I know many examples of dogs who, after their masters passed, experienced such loneliness that they never recovered. There's the famous account of the Japanese dog that used to meet his owner at the train station in Shibuya, Tokyo, every night after work and walk home with him. When the man died at his place of work and never came home again, the dog continued to meet the train for fifteen years until he finally rejoined his master in heaven. A friend of mine who had AIDS couldn't take care of his dog anymore so he gave the dog to a good family. The dog ran away and walked thirty miles back to my friend's house. My friend returned him to the new owner, and soon after that, my friend died. His dog died within two hours.

When we get back from a walk on the beach Terry will sometimes sit on the balcony for hours, gazing at the horizon. What does she see? Can she see into the underlying cycles of time—or beyond them? Does she see spirit guides? Dog playmates? Relatives who have passed on? Is she seeing God? Is this why she likes to be perched atop something high, giving her a grander vista? When the wind blows Terry goes into a kind of reverie, as though she is receiving messages from other dimensions.

What does Terry think when she chases the shadow of a seagull flying overhead? Does she think that the shadow is solid, or is she pouncing on a moment that once was but is no more? She's interested beyond measure in shadows, particularly moving shadows, and I'd love to know why.

When Terry plays outside on the beach with other friends, she checks in every twenty minutes or so to see that I am still there, to remind me that she's fine, to stretch, to yawn, and to look up at me. Is she trying to say, I will be patient until you join me in the interplay of darkness and light, when I can show you what you're missing? She bounds into the sunlit ocean waves and buries her face in the salty water, only to leap into the air at the shadow of a dive-bombing pelican. Who is this little sprite of a fur person? When I walk with her and she scampers under the pilings of people's seaside homes I revel in her unbounded freedom, and I am filled with the wonder of knowing that I was holding and cuddling her the night before.

Some friends say I'm losing my mind over the intimacy I feel with this dog. Sometimes I think they are right. I have lived with dogs all my life—golden retrievers, German shepherds, mutts, malamutes, Australian shepherds, huskies, always good-sized dogs—but this is the first time I've had a terrier in my adult life.

I did have a little terrier when I was small. Her name was Trixie. Perhaps that's why I have inherited Terry now. Maybe Terry is Trixie, come around again. She certainly has the same traits, but then again, as a terrier, she would. Somehow I find comfort in the knowledge that we are all like terriers, or snowflakes—with a beauty in common that is only enhanced by our uniqueness. Yet that same image adds to my anxiety, for most humans fight and fear our differences. We are all one under God, yet we will always be part of the puzzle of suffering until we find a remedy for separation, not only from each other but, more profoundly, from what Native Americans call the "Great Spirit All There Is."

Terry

*My Mistress Mother knows I can see things that she cannot. All animals can. We can **hear** colors and **see** sounds. Red, orange, yellow, green, blue, indigo, and violet: Each color has a frequency, and we canines can hear those vibrations. We also **see** how sounds vibrate and what voices **look** like. Our ears and eyes are fine-tuned instruments, just like our other senses. I know when the ocean is disturbed or even angry. I hear and see nature because I am nature. But MM is not in that state of mind, poor thing. She is not a princess of simplicity like I am.*

That peaceful way of living is there for all of us, but my MM and her friends are too busy taking care of things they think they have to do in a day. This is why they can't sleep well at night. It's also why my friends and

I sleep so much. We don't feel stressed. We're peaceful. We see things in our sleep-state but we don't really care if we remember them or not. We know we are perfect just as we are, which is why we have such dignity. Humans marvel at our talent for forgiveness, yet we feel we have nothing to forgive. We know everything is exactly as it should be. Sometimes humans try our patience and upset nature in general. They should be especially careful of what they're dumping into the ocean because someday the ocean is going to get very mad and hit back. That could really happen, of course; it already did, a long time ago.

As far as shadows are concerned, we know all about them. We know that all of human suffering is based on shadows: shadows in themselves, and shadows in others. We canines play with shadows because we know they are just part of the game. All of life is a game, so we live to be happy. The shadowy fears that humans see as causes for their anxiety are really only parts of themselves. We play with these things.

Humans don't understand pecking order, either. They don't realize that they have lived before and will live again; a being who was once leader of the pack may soon be a puppy, clinging to life. We understand that. It makes us humble.

We see many dimensions, including past, present, and future, and we know they are all happening simultaneously. We know that people have invented time. We know that living in every single moment is all there is. It's so simple, yet my MM and the rest of the humans don't get it. How can they have time to do those things that upset them when there's no such thing as time? I sometimes think they invented time so they'd always have something to worry about. I don't like to watch my MM and her friends fret about silly things, like what to wear. That's why I sometimes give my MM a hard time about putting on my store-bought coat before going out into the snow and rain. I have my own coat. I am completely naked, but I am also fully clothed and protected.

People are often surprised when they feel our little cold noses, but do they know why our noses are so cold? We are regulated by nature to be warm inside but our noses are never really hot unless we're taking on a sickness. When my MM is brushing her teeth with her jammies on and she's leaning over the sink, I like to go and stick my cold nose against her butt so she'll shriek with surprise.

Speaking of butts, I remember a time when my MM was giving a dinner party and she served spare ribs. I begged and begged for those leftover ribs, and finally she gave them to me. I ate all the meat off of them and then I ate the bones and I was very sick the next day. Nobody should ever feed us bones that splinter, no matter how much we beg. Our bones have to be big and thick, like they were when we were wolves and hunted in packs. My Mistress Mom was very worried about me. I wasn't just shivering, I really didn't feel good, and when she saw something was wrong she took me to the doctor. I remember the doctor spent the entire day up my butt getting the splintered bones out of my insides. If they hadn't come out, I could have been punctured, which is not a good thing for anybody.

I've heard my MM and her friends wonder why dogs smell each other's butts. We learn a lot from sniffing butts. *We can tell what our friends have eaten, where they've been, and even whether or not they've been well. We can also tell whether or not they are nice or threatening. I've noticed a lot of people now call each other "assholes" on TV, so perhaps humans are beginning to see that we're right about the importance of butts.*

Even though we dogs are perfect, we do have some problems. For example, when males of our species go around lifting their legs and peeing to mark their territory, this is not a good thing. Maybe marking territory is something we learned from the humans, since we've been bonded to them for so long. Perhaps by setting a good example, and not peeing on each other, people could stop our males from doing that too. Nothing belongs to anybody, it all belongs to everybody, and all of us and all of it belong to the Great Spirit God anyway. We all just **use** *territory. Nobody* **owns** *it.*

If any of my friends come along to eat out of my dish, I let them do it and I will always let them do it, although I suppose if I was starving, that might be another story. But instead of people spending all that stuff they call money on weapons to protect themselves, I think they should spend that money to feed everybody; then nobody would be angry or frightened in the first place.

*I heard on MM's TV that a human child dies every seven seconds from not having enough food, and that there are eight hundred million starving children in the world. I'm glad I am my MM's dog when I hear that, but shouldn't people's children be treated as well as their dogs? No wonder so many people are angry. When I feel angry it's because I'm afraid. Humans will do terrible things to keep from being afraid. And why are they afraid? They're afraid that they don't have enough. And why are they afraid they don't have enough? They're afraid that if they don't have enough they will die. But the truth of the matter is, nothing and nobody ever dies, and **that** is one of the biggest secrets of all. Nothing ever dies; it just changes form. And that's the Big Truth.*

Shirley

The producers tell me that the movie in Ireland may very well start shooting this summer. I've checked everywhere for ways to get past the quarantine laws but I'm not making any headway. The most plausible advice I've been given is to go to Paris and find a veterinarian who will keep Terry for a few weeks and say she's been there longer, certifying that she is rabies-free. Then we could travel through the Chunnel to England.

Terry is used to me; I don't want her to have to adjust to being away from me for a long time, assuming she even could. And to be honest, I suffer from canine separation anxiety myself. I never thought this would happen to me.

During my various travels around the world, I never liked to go with anyone else. I liked to be able to pick up at a moment's notice or stay in one place until I had had enough of it. Life was a spontaneous, unpredictable adventure. I traveled light and unencumbered. As my father often said, "He travels fastest who travels alone."

When I have had to leave people I loved, I knew that they and I would grieve, but that eventually we would get on with our lives. I knew, despite what we might think, we were not dependent on each other. Not so with Terry. I'm now dependent on the love she brings out in me. I don't want to be away from the reminder of that love.

The producer of the movie now says we'll begin shooting in May, just after Easter. Maybe I can put "dependent on Terry being with me" into my contract, and let the producer sort out the details.

Terry

Perhaps I should play the Hollywood game too. Here are my demands: Put me in MM's contract, overseas first-class tickets all the way.

Shirley

There is nothing sadder for a dog than being left alone, and many dog experts believe that there is nothing comparable in human experience to the degree of loneliness experienced by an isolated dog. Terry needs to speak and be spoken to. She needs to touch and be touched. She needs to love and be loved. I know this is true for humans too, so why won't we acknowledge it the way dogs do?

Terry can live happily and at ease in two worlds: hers and mine. That makes her much more clever than I am, but I am making some progress. Terry may have levels of perception that I can't comprehend, but as far as the five senses go, in some ways she is better equipped than I am, and in others, she's not. A dog, for example, has one taste bud for every six of ours, which is why dogs can eat the same food every day and seem content. I know dogs have favorite foods and I would gladly become a cook for Terry, but she is happy with whatever I give her, except for fruit. She doesn't like fruit.

A dog's vision is comparable to that of a human being, although it's not quite as good. Dogs' eyes are very much more sensitive to movement than ours. And yet dogs can be easily spooked by something they see. One day, Terry barked at a statue of Buddha in my house for hours. I wonder why. Was she frightened, or did she feel something familiar, and want to communicate?

Dogs have much better hearing than we humans do; they can hear sounds four times farther away. Terry is constantly freezing in her tracks, one paw up, indicating that she's heard something outside of my range. Terry's ears also move independently, so she can get a better directional fix than I can. A dog can locate the source of a sound in six hundredths of a second. That's why I so often see Terry stop to listen and then immediately go racing off in a specific direction.

And of course it's well-known that dogs are able to detect higher pitched sounds than we are. That's why Terry always seems to find chipmunks and squirrels and other ground rodents that are emitting high-frequency signals beyond the reach of the human ear. Terry can hear a storm coming long before I can, or maybe she just smells the electricity in the air. I wonder if she can hear fish swimming.

A dog's sense of touch is also extremely sensitive. Terry's entire body is covered with nerve endings. Dogs sense air flowing through extremely sensitive hairs located above their eyes, on their faces, or below the jaw. That might be why Terry raises her head when she stops and focuses far out on the ocean. When she raises her head, this also enhances her ability to smell. Maybe she smells the dolphins and the whales.

The relationship between emotions and sensory experiences allows dogs to be in constant touch with their emotional core, which is why we see dogs live through such a wide range of emotions in any one day. Because a dog's sensory world is so rich, it's in constant interplay with its own emotional world.

I think as humans our best test of morality may be our attitude toward those who are at our mercy, namely animals. I'm more and more convinced that the love I have for a dog is as important or greater than any love I could have for a man or woman because it's a completely voluntary and selfless love. And Terry returns my love so openly, so fiercely, that I begin to see what is possible between human beings. It's funny to think that I've been so interested in life on other planets when I haven't even begun to understand the alien life on my own world.

Terry

We are taking one last quick beach romp before we go to the ranch for Easter. I dash once more into the waves and chase the shadows of a squadron of seagulls. I decide not to dig out picnics abandoned on the sand, and I don't lap up any salt water even though I'm thirsty; MM says it's bad for me. Soon we have to leave for the airport, so MM is turning around to go back to our beach house. Now when she tosses wet sand into the air it hits her in the face, because the wind is blowing the wrong way. She'll get tired of that very quickly, and will walk faster so we can get ready to go on the plane. I'll be good and tired and ready to go to sleep under the seat, dreaming of dolphins because I know they bring good luck.

Airports are my favorite places to observe how humans react to me. My MM has a little rolling case for me so she can pull me like a piece of luggage. Whenever *we get to a waiting lounge or the Red Carpet place, she opens the case and people are surprised to see my little head pop out. I'm careful not to scamper around where food is being served, because that's against health code rules. But everybody always wants to play with me. You would think I had landed from a friendly planet and no one had ever seen my kind before when I come out of my case and twinkle up to people.*

We are leaving for New Mexico. There has been a terror alert, and even though I am sometimes called "Terry the Terror," I can't understand why I have to keep going in and out of my case. I go through the beeping screening arch, and then they make me get out of my case, and then people in uniforms feel my stomach and rummage around in my empty case. I see my MM is also being felt by a female in uniform; she is taking off MM's shoes, and asking her if there is metal in her bra.

I am immediately attracted to one of the big, strong female security agents because she seems so stern, so I scamper over to her and jump up to be petted. She is so mad, she steps back and shouts "Get down! Get down!" My

MM replies, "Oh, she's just a dog, she's just a little play-mate." The security agent leads MM into a little cubicle and I hear her say "I want to see everything that's underneath your clothes." I don't know what's going on because I'm left outside while other people try to pet me. What did I do wrong? I look under the cubicle as MM lifts her skirt and shirt. The lady does not touch her, but she is not being nice. I can see why I chose to make her happier.

Now we are on the plane to New Mexico. We are all settled in our spaces. I am under the seat in front of my Mistress Mother but my little doggie bag case sticks out just a little bit. The male flight attendant is bending over us looking very closely at my case. My MM says "Well, it's got a tag that says 'Approved by America West.'" The attendant says, "It doesn't fit." I realize we might have a problem. He bends over and tries to push me farther under the seat. He is hurting my back so I growl. A few other people in first class hear me. Up to now they must have thought I was a piece of luggage. I see them looking over. The attendant keeps saying, "It doesn't fit," and every time he tries to push me in farther I growl. My MM is getting embarrassed because she doesn't want to feel she is getting special treatment, but she hates what he's doing to me.

Another flight attendant comes over. Because she's a female I think everything will be all right. But when my MM shows her the America West approval tag, the male attendant says, "That doesn't matter if the case doesn't fit." The female attendant doesn't seem to know what to do.

The other passengers begin to speak up. "C'mon, let's go, it doesn't matter." But the male flight attendant just stands there looking at me. There is a lot of commotion because now everyone knows what is going on and my MM won't give up and he won't give up. Half an hour goes by while other people in uniforms come on and off the plane. There is more confusion. Now the pilot is coming out. I hear him ask, "What's the dog's name?" My MM says to him, "Terry. She and I have always flown America West because this case is approved." He asks, "You don't fly Southwest?" She says, "No, they don't allow dogs." He says, "Do you take Terry everywhere?" My MM answers, "Yes."

The pilot is reaching down and rolling my case into the aisle. "Okay Terry," he says, "we'll take you into the cockpit." His voice sounds so sweet.

The pilot has taken me into the cockpit and now he's even giving me a treat. I wish I could twirl for him, but of course I can't get out of my case. I know my MM is probably fuming in her seat, but I know she's also grateful to the nice pilot.

Everybody who was trying to help leaves the plane and now I feel the familiar push of the plane taking off. I know it's time for me to be quiet and sleep. I can feel my MM decide to call America West by a new name—from now on she will call it America Worst!

Shirley

Once, when I was on a Christmas vacation in Palm Beach, Florida, I lost Terry. We were staying with some friends in a beautiful home, but Terry did not have dogs to play with. There were too many sophisticated grown-ups around, so Terry decided to go down to the beach by herself. She was missing for two hours. I was frantic, but I have a council of angels, and I asked them where Terry had gone. They directed me south. I walked along the beach until I came to a country club, where one of the attendants told me that a little white-and-black terrier had followed a group of kids to the country club, and then an elderly gentleman, who was worried about the dog, took her home with him. He pointed me in the direction of the man's house.

I walked over to it, and there was Terry, having the time of her life playing with a bunch of other dogs. She had her dog tag on, but of course the two telephone numbers listed were in California and in New Mexico, so the man couldn't contact me. Terry, being of a mind of timelessness, had no idea that her being gone would worry me. I have relied on my council of angels ever since. In fact I believe we always play and walk with our angels, and they always try to get our attention when we're too busy thinking and worrying.

Terry

Humans should play more for no reason, like the angels do. Angels play in all kinds of ways. For example, since I am an earth angel I love to charge at nothing in the middle of the night, and sometimes it wakes my MM up, but perhaps she should be more aware of the night sounds. Perhaps she should be more aware of the glory of the moon. I bay at the moon and gaze at the stars, hoping that she will take the cue and do it more herself. I want my MM's angel child to come out and play more. I love to charge at thunder when a rainstorm comes up. To me, the weather is entertainment, but it is also a reflection of turmoil in human emotions. We natural beings know that nature follows consciousness. It's nothing to be afraid of, except when people don't understand that nature will be

61

strange and chaotic when they are. I love to return from my charging at the night to nuzzle into my MM's neck and tell her to be careful how she treats nature. She giggles when my nose is too cold, but I'm not sure she understands my point about nature. I nuzzle up against her shoulder and cuddle myself into her arms to keep her warm and hope she gets what I'm trying to teach her. Sometimes we watch movies, especially Stuart Little *and* Stuart Little II. *I love those two. Perhaps my being a rat terrier has something to do with it.*

Once my MM took me to a ball in celebration of a ballet company, and she said the theme of the ball was Cinderella. I remembered having seen the minds of children when they read Cinderella. It was really nice. I liked the ball that Cinderella went to and found her prince, so I loved the idea of attending with MM. But when we arrived at the ball, three big people dressed in rat suits greeted us. Even their faces looked exactly like rats, whiskers and all, because they were wearing some kind of rat hoods. They were so big there was no way I could *charge at them. MM said not to worry but I ran away and hid in the Cinderella carriage. Everybody laughed and said I was cute, but I didn't feel cute. I was afraid the human rats would charge at **me**. I tried to shiver like I do when I want attention but I was too scared.*

After that terrifying experience, I had to ask myself why I attack anything. I think it might be because it runs away, and I love to catch things that run away. But as far as hurting anything, I would rather roll over on my back and be adorable with my feet up in the air, inviting whoever or whatever to do what they want with me. Maybe even rats, especially if they are as big as they were that day!

I know my MM loves to watch me sitting content-edly in my world of other-dimensional communication. Being in many worlds simultaneously takes silence and concentration. I practice this every day. I wish MM would take more time for silence and concentration. Still, I don't mind being distracted when my MM comes over to me after an upsetting phone call and just hugs me. That helps her. She has also learned to make little sniffing sounds in my ear and all over my face, like other dogs do with me. It makes me think that she is finally, on some level, entering my world of wisdom.

*When it comes to just being, I know that my MM is more capable of this than most people because her practical needs are being met. Other people have their work, their pressures, children to feed, chores, and other things that go along with busy human lives. MM is past all that so she can afford to "just be" although she still needs to **be** better. I know that many of my furry friends wish their owners would take time to just be too. If they would just take an hour, even if it meant getting up earlier, my furry friends would get up with them and help them "just be," silently connecting with all there is.*

This business of just being is really what they call "profound." It's especially important now for humans because what they have made of their lives is really not natural. Once they sit with a twinkling leaf that shimmers in the sun, or watch a sparrow bounce around in the seeds, or get involved with water flowing over a rock, once they see the importance of that, they will begin to absorb that "being" information into their lives. That's what I do for my Mistress Mother; that's what all pets do for their masters and mistresses. When they're with us their blood pressure drops and their hearts become healthier. We serve a great purpose to humans just by being ourselves. This is why we are magical to them.

I love to be mischievous and bawdy with MM. She wouldn't like a dull and placid dog anyway. I love to make her laugh, even with my bathroom humor. I love to have her watch me when I go out for my morning poop. In the middle of my search for a good place I love to suddenly squat down and pretend to notice a cactus needle in my hind leg. I lift my leg in the middle of a poop just so she'll know I'm capable of multitasking. This always makes her laugh.

I'm very respectful of my Mistress Mom when she's on an important phone call, or when she is reading a script, or when she is writing something. She doesn't realize it but I am helping her write these very words. But when I sense a break in her focus, I run from the other side of the room and jump into her lap so she'll think I'm just a dog. This surprises her, and sometimes shocks her, but then she always laughs and cuddles me. When she cuddles me, I don't know who gets more pleasure, she or I. So it's not that I'm an even-keeled, entertaining soul-being. I can also be a very unpredictable one. Whatever works. But I also want her to get back to her writing because she has reached an age when she is really looking at the meaning of life in a deep way, which is why she loves me so much.

Shirley

In the *Mahabharata,* the celebrated Indian epic poem written more than 2,000 years ago, a great emperor is making a trek to the Himalayas, accompanied by his four brothers and his wife, when a small dog attaches himself to the retinue. As the trip progresses, one by one the members of the royal party fall victim to the hardships of the road, and die, until the emperor's only remaining companion is his adopted dog. When they reach the end of their journey at the gates of heaven, the King of the Heavenly Gates comes to greet the emperor in regal and godly splendor. He then says, "But the dog cannot come with you. You will achieve immortality equal to mine, but you must leave the dog." The emperor replies, "No, I can't, he is devoted to me; he has been with me all along this arduous journey." And the King of the Heavenly Gates says, "There is no place in heaven for persons with dogs. Abandon the dog." Calmly but firmly the emperor responds, "I will under no circumstances abandon this dog just to achieve happiness for myself." So the King of the Heavenly Gates tries to convince him one last time, "If you give up the dog you will acquire the world of heaven. You've already given up your brothers and wife. You have obtained heaven through your very own deeds. You have already abandoned everything else. How can you be so confused as to not give up a dog?" The emperor still refuses, saying he abandoned his wife and brothers because they were already dead, but he will not abandon the living dog. At that point the dog reveals himself to be none other than the great god Dharma, god of cosmic order and moral principle, who tells the emperor he has passed this final test of his virtue.

Of course dog spelled backward is God.

Terry

Because of what happened on America Worst, my MM has been talking about finding someone who owns an airplane. I don't know if she means marrying someone who has an airplane, or finding a very close companion-friend who has an airplane. What would happen if that friend with the airplane wanted to share the bed with my Mistress Mom and me? I think that could be very difficult, so I hope airport security relaxes enough so that we can have our life together without a man involved. She doesn't know that I can read the pillow she has on her bed that says, "The more I know about MEN the more I love my Dog." When I read this it makes me feel secure in our future.

When strangers come to my MM's home or to her movie trailer, I always jump up in their laps and kiss them as though I have known them all their lives, which I have. That makes them feel very loved. When I play princess I want all the attention I can get any way, and of course I want everyone to love me too. So everybody wins as long as it's not women with black dresses and pearls, who are afraid that dog hair is something that no outfit needs. However, most strangers are so happy with the attention and love I lavish on them that they don't really look down to see what their clothes look like. Anyway, no outfit is complete without dog hair. Basically, dog hairs are threads of love from heaven.

When we arrive at a hotel, I know what the concierge's uniforms look like now, so while my MM is checking in I go right over to the concierge and jump up, lick his face, and gently nip his nose. When he takes all my Mistress Mom's bags up to the room, I run around in circles and help him unpack the bags. Sometimes I even drag out my MM's undies so that he gets a big laugh. After I have connected with the concierge, I know he'll want to come and take me for walks when my mom is busy. He'll also talk to me about other people in the hotel, but I would never divulge those secrets. He gives me treats too.

Since I go everywhere with my Mistress Mom, I'm at her side when she works on a movie. The word gets around when I am on a movie set. I find myself loving the lights. I gravitate to them because then people can see me do my tricks, they can see me be adorable. I also like the Teamsters, who are a union. I like the Teamsters because they let me into their trailer, let me watch football, let me chase the players on the TV screen, and give me lots of treats. In fact, they even get extra popcorn and lots of food for me from the catering table. So I am a Teamster dog when I'm on the set.

Once while working on a movie MM had really bad shoulder pain. She wrenched her shoulder during one of her workouts, and she was writhing in agony down on the floor of her trailer. I jumped up on her shoulder and hugged it. I hugged it very tight. Then I ran and got my favorite Teamster and he gave my MM some medicine and she was all better. And now every morning when I see her down on the floor doing her exercises, I run up to her and I hug her shoulder and her arm, because I don't want her to hurt herself. I hope she understands that's what I'm doing.

The Teamsters take turns taking me on walks, and bringing me food from the catering tables. They are really tired by the end of the day, but they still come in early the next morning when my MM is in the makeup trailer to play with me all over again. I know I'm a girl, but I feel like one of them. Sometimes I wait in my Mistress Mom's trailer for her to come back from a scene; when she does she wears these funny things on her head that she calls wigs, but they look like strange hats to me. Sometimes she has blond-wig hats, sometimes she has long brown-wig hats, and sometimes she has gray-wig hats. Sometimes when she hasn't had time to visit the hairdresser, her own hair is the color of the gray-wig hat. But now I'm telling secrets that my Mistress Mom doesn't want anybody else to know.

I also like to watch her in the makeup chair because she doesn't wear makeup in real life. She puts on makeup to become "the character." When she becomes the character, she plays with me in a different way because she thinks she's different.

I see my MM's thoughts in images and I see them in colors. When she says we're going for a ride in the car, she's picturing that ride in the car so that's why I run to the car, because that's what I see in her mind. Sometimes when she's been on the set I stare at her when she comes back into the trailer to be with me, so I can see the scene that she's just done because it's still in her mind. I can see the other actors, I can see the lights (which I wish I were in), and I can see the costumes and her silly wig hats.

In long-ago times we didn't need language. We communicated with each other using thoughts. It was much clearer because we didn't get confused or manipulated by words. I still have that long-ago talent, and I wish humans did too. They really need to get back to basics.

Shirley

An architect friend of mine once told me he always had to leave his dog at home when he went to work, where he was busy with blueprints and scale models. When he came home his dog would simply stare at him, focusing intently on his forehead. A pet communicator told him that the dog was entering into his master's mind. He was reading the plans, and considering the images of the model buildings. Once he had read the architect's mind he could relax, but not until he knew what his master had been doing all day.

I try to communicate with Terry regularly to improve my thought transference. I'm trying to do the same thing with flowers and birds and trees—and yes, even rocks. When I lived with the Masai in Kenya, Africa, the white hunters told me that the Masai were very accomplished at projecting and receiving each other's thoughts. They didn't need telephones or e-mail. With their minds they also tuned in to the movements of animals as well as the cycles of nature and the weather.

Terry

I wonder if my MM knows that all living beings on our earth are created from the same thing. I know that my MM understands she doesn't own me, and because she doesn't treat me like a possession, I don't think of her as an owner. Other dogs and animals and trees and flowers are equal to my MM and me, although she and I do have a special connection. The more thought intelligence my MM communicates to me, the more I can respond with. I love the idea that she knows how wise I am. I know she knows that I'm a royal terrier, that I'm different from Spooky and Sheba and Daisy and Sandy and the other dogs on the ranch—but she also knows I'm her teacher.

Sometimes I look away when my MM looks into my eyes, because I don't want to confuse her by letting her learn too fast. Humans have to learn according to their limited pace. I can feel her wondering what it's like to be in my little body. I know she's trying to sense what it feels like to have four feet and fur and a cold nose. I wish she would wonder what it's like to have my cosmic wisdom. I love it when she explains the reasons why she's asking me to do something: like I don't already know! If she says I can't have any more kibble because I'll get fat, I understand for goodness' sake. But if she just says I can't have any more kibble, then I'll keep begging. I also like it when she makes deals with me. That way I know that she understands we are equals. When I don't want to have my bath and she says "I will give you a treat if you will come up nicely and let me bathe you in the sink," of course I know it's a deal. But I love getting extra treats too. I love it when she tries to think like I think. That's the best fun of all.

One of my favorite moments comes when we sit quietly together, look out at the mountains, and watch the rain start to fall. It's even better when it snows. Ooooh, I love to play in the snow. I love to bite the soft flakes and taste a little of the heaven they came from.

*My MM knows that I am the treasure in her heart, which is why I bring her to tears. Even though she can't hear me speak of all these things, I can hear **her** speak and I understand everything in her mind and her heart. I know that God is there inside her and soon she will learn to communicate with every little thing that God is.*

Shirley

Here it is, Easter weekend, and I'm sitting here with Terry in my ranch house in New Mexico contemplating all I've learned from books, from working in movies, from art, from channeling, from living, from my walk on the Camino, and from reading the Bible. I watch the wind breezily cleanse everything. Could it be that I did not really feel up to emotionally accepting what I knew with my intellect until Terry came into my life? It's very synchronistic that these thoughts are coalescing into words on an Easter weekend. Christ, who died for our sins, asked us to turn the other cheek again and again. That's what dogs do with humans. But can humans really do that with dogs? Or with each other? Is that what the next big planetary transformation will be all about: the ability to turn the other cheek?

The laws of nature are harmonious and we are defiling nature. We say nature is cruel, but we define cruelty even as we cause it. Would we be more balanced if we allowed nature to be balanced? The mere fact that I, at my age, still ask these questions proves to me that I have not understood one simple truth: that we and nature are part of that which gives us the feeling of love. I understand it more now because of a little dog, but still there are questions that haunt me about the world and God. What is real—that which we perceive to be real or that which we cannot see? Are Heaven and God and Spirit more real than the world around us?

I am beginning to realize that the "real" reality is the one I don't altogether accept. The "real" reality is what I know deep inside, but continue to separate myself from: the spirit within, which has little to do with religion. I have come to understand this most profoundly through my relationship with a dog, which most religions claim has no soul.

Terry has strategies for survival and basic needs,

but these are not violent, or angry, or full of guilt or self-judgment; they just *are*. My happiness with her makes me cry. Why? Why do we humans cry when we are ecstatically happy, when we are rewarded with something we've always wanted? Do we feel we don't deserve it? Or do we cry in moments of happiness because we know so many others don't feel this way?

If I look at the world and I see it as sad and ravaged and polluted, as competitive and dangerous and hostile—basically, I would have to say, insane—that will be my only experience of it. I will therefore create a world without meaning. As I look at Terry I can't believe she lives in such a world. She seems to have no purpose except just to BE. THAT is her meaning. And that is what she's giving me: the right just to be. But just to be what?

Why should connecting to the spirit that is our basic nature be so complicated? I know we are not physical beings looking for a soul; we are soul beings who should have the right simply to be happy while we are physical. I watch Terry, totally absorbed in the sound of

a bird, or so delighted by a toy that she will sponta-
neously leap on it and bring it to me, as if to say play is
important: "Play with me. Shake my toy." She loves to
hunt and to run; she loves to keep her senses alive. She
didn't create war. She didn't create taxes. She didn't create an addictive technological culture. She didn't create
pollution, or airplane crashes, or violence, or terrorism,
or dope, or even meaninglessness. In this world as I perceive it, Terry brings happiness just by being. I wish I
could be that way.

Terry

My MM and I have been together through many lifetimes. As I said, when we lived in ancient Egypt together, I was the god Anubis and MM was a minor princess. What I didn't reveal was the story of a strange, remarkably intelligent king who shared that time with us. He didn't look like other human beings. He had big eyes and gray skin and a face shaped like a triangle. He was a very powerful and kind king, who knew many things that humans did not. Humans worshiped him, and sometimes were afraid of him, because he came from out of the sky.

This king taught Egyptians about the ways of nature, the stars and cosmic numbers, and other celestial matters. He said he came from his world on a silent, round airboat. He said I should take care of the princess and teach her now and always through time, and never to forget that. When he died, there was a great ceremony, and he was buried next to his airboat deep in the ground.

Just a few weeks ago my MM was watching a television program about a KGB Russian intelligence team that had uncovered the old king and his airboat in Egypt. It was all very top secret, but he looked exactly like the king I remembered! The KGB people believed he was from Orion and said the Egyptians in those ancient days wrote about how he had come to teach them many things. I noticed that my MM was very interested in the program and cuddled me closely with familiar feeling. I am keeping my promise to the king, because royal celestial agreements are very important. I am continuing my teachings with MM now, and I'm hopeful she'll get it this time.

Sometimes when my MM and I travel by airplane and struggle to get where we're going I wonder why we can't go in a silent airboat like the king's. Things are so rudimentary now. But I have to continue to adjust.

Shirley

My land in New Mexico speaks to me when I walk it. As I walk with the ranch dogs I feel its power and knowledge. These ancient rocks and flat-topped mesas remind me that this land, now nearly 7,000 feet high, was once under water.

Years ago I was told by a shaman that a dog would come, a spirit dog with one blue eye and one dark eye, and that he would circle the ranch house for a few months and then come in and claim his right to protect it. That's exactly what happened. Spooky is a mixed breed, the one male in this harem of females. Not far behind him is Sheba, a mix of German shepherd, malamute, and husky. Magnificently dignified, she can also be short-tempered, which is her prerogative as the oldest female. Daisy is an Australian shepherd collie, kept young by Sandy, an obstreperous, delightful, and totally untrainable retriever. And of course there's Terry the Princess Terrier, who never leaves my side.

The dogs and I are walking among the ghosts and spirits of the past. There are Indian ruins under our feet, where tribal people traded turquoise and beads for livestock and grain. A stream runs alongside our mountain rim-walking, as we make our way toward the petroglyphs, carvings in the rocks that some say are over three thousand years old. I wonder if I lived here long ago. And was Terry with me then? Could that be why I was drawn back to call it my real home?

Terry seems to understand the ancient energy. She leaves no rock uninvestigated, as though listening within them for messages from bygone voices.

I remember J. Krishnamurti, the Indian sage and writer from New Delhi who returned from a long walk not unlike this one and reported that he had not had one single thought along the way. Oh, to quiet my mind like that! First I'd need to dissolve negative thoughts, then anxious thoughts, then regretful thoughts, and let's not forget guilty thoughts. I can't really imagine an extended stay in a no-thought state, but on long walks I do feel my mind settling into a state of detached composure, the way I imagine Terry, or a hawk wheeling overhead, or even a boulder might feel. And sometimes when Terry freezes, gazing at a point I can't see, I try to enter that space and as I do, an extraordinary sense of peace comes over me. In that moment I feel that no matter what madness we humans bring upon ourselves, the animals, the sky, and the mountains will watch in dignified silence, hoping we will come to our senses.

According to Buddhism, life is an illusion, a dream we have created in our three-dimensional "reality." Am I recognizing in Terry that she is having her own divine reality, which is infinitely less judgmental than my own?

Buddhists say we live in a state of blissful nothingness but we don't know it, because we think that what we have created is real. Have I limited my body's eyes to seeing only those images that I think are real? If so, then the illusion I've created is like a curtain hiding the real reality from me. I know something about creating illusion, because that's my business. I know something about creating reality too, because when I play a part, that's my task. But image-making is not the same as seeing the truth.

Is the ravaged world far away from me also my own creation? When I turn on CNN or the news shows on Sunday, am I creating those journalists and those politicians and those people who speak about how much trouble we are in? Am I encouraging them to do that in my dream? If my thoughts are negative and fearful, perhaps that is the reality I will create. If each of us in our varying states of distress and fearfulness creates our own world, it's a wonder we're not in more collective trouble!

Perhaps on his walk Krishnamurti touched upon what Terry has known since she was born. Maybe Terry is not seeing the world as I see it, my garden as I see it, this land as I see it, my clothing as I see it, or even her toys as I see them. Perhaps what I sense in her is that she

is seeing beyond image-making to the Big Truth. As I
get older and spend more time with Terry, I want to see
what would happen if I changed my illusions. Is that
possible? If I radically shifted my illusions would I perceive the world in a whole new way? Could Terry and I
ever see the same sunset? I believe she sees more than I
do, and sees it more deeply, but maybe even that thought
is just part of the dream I'm having. Maybe I've even
created this little dog who is my profound teacher.

I don't want to leave Terry to make a movie because
she gives me peace and laughter and puts me in touch
with how different she is from goal-oriented moviemak-
ers. In the main, the movies my industry makes cater to
the lowest instincts in people. Of course movies have to
make profit, but by glorifying violence and preying on
people's fears they're just perpetuating the problem. I'm
beginning to fear a breakdown of society. When people
believe their governments don't tell them the truth, different factions may take matters into their own hands and
fight each other. We are so afraid of terrorism from abroad

that we may fight and kill each other right here, at home. But when I stop walking and gaze into Terry's eyes, she gives me a deep sense of comfort—telling me that everything is happening just as it should in order for us to learn who we really are. So why do we have to learn with such suffering and fear?

Terry

MM watches the news all the time because she wants to know how much trouble people are in. People are in trouble because they're not watching the news within themselves. MM is really concerned but I also think she sees the situation in the world as a kind of horrible entertainment, but that's because humans are a horrible entertainment within themselves. Many of her friends tell her they've stopped looking at the news and they don't even read their papers anymore because everything is so disturbing. But ignorance never solves problems, and so many are in self-ignorance. My MM is not one to go into denial. She wants to know, but doesn't know where the answers are. Well, that's easy, they're within herself.

MM and I are sitting on a hill overlooking our house. The trees are talking to me and each one has a story to tell. These juniper trees have a long lineage, and their ancestors have experienced many things. They tell me they know that the insects living among them are not pleasant for humans, but they have a place in the lives of the trees. The juniper insects might even contribute to the gin that humans make from juniper berries. I've never had a drink of that stuff, but I've seen many of MM's friends become funnier when they drink that insect juniper juice! So you see everything has a place in life. However, that gin juice may have too important a place in some people's lives.

The tall ponderosa pine trees are telling me that humans cut many of their ancestors down in order to make homes. They say they have no judgment about that because they are happy to serve the needs of people, and to shelter them from nature. They know their ancestor trees never died; they now live in the ceilings and walls of people's homes.

The birds darting in and out of the trees tell me what they have seen humans do from their vantage point in the sky. They love the insects in the trees because they make good meals. They tell me about the secrets of the air and their knowledge of flight. They are happy to have served as models for the airplane, but they don't like what airplanes do when they drop things that kill trees and people.

As I look over everything, I love being with MM just doing nothing but hearing all the stories of the life around me. All living things have a history . . . his-story, her-story, its-story—and they see things from their own perspectives. Every living thing has something to say, some story to tell. So when MM asks what is real I want to tell her that perception is the only reality until all life becomes one again—didn't one of those humans call it The Unified Field Theory?

Everything has energy, and all of it has a purpose. Some energies may be denser than others, but they all have a reason for being. Nothing is evil. That is only a human perception. Humans like to think there is a duality in the world, and they call it Good and Evil. Because they believe that, they have made a world that seems to prove that this is true. But it isn't. Humans don't want to consider that there is no such thing as Good and Evil, though, because they are used to living in that duality. It seems to give them a reason to be alive—to conquer "evil" when evil is what's thumping away in their own minds and hearts. Even their Bible says, "Thou shalt not eat of the fruit of the tree of 'knowledge' of good and evil," but they kept on eating that faulty knowledge.

Nature doesn't think that way. We animals don't think that way, mostly because we haven't been taught to think that way. We know that what humans call evil is just an expression of inner confusion, and a disconnect from the Divine that I see all around us. I'm digging in the dirt now because I don't want to get confused by people thinking, but I can feel Mother Earth growing tired of being used as a stage upon which this drama of Good and Evil is being played out.

*Whenever humans feel love within themselves they usually can't take it for very long and they accuse themselves and each other of being self-centered. But if they saw the love **and** the light energy inside themselves, their* *perspective on the outside world would change, and it would actually reflect what they see in themselves.*

The wars in the world are the wars that start within people, long before anyone attacks anyone else. These inner wars create the outer disturbances. I wish they could see that love is their human inheritance.

I stop digging and sit beside MM again. As we rest here on this hill I wonder if Mother Earth will ultimately decide to erupt and restore balance between herself and the life that walks across her stage. Maybe in the light of creation she will want to start all over again. I would hate to see that happen because people could be such beautiful beings if they only knew it. We fur people know who we are and if people don't hurt us we'll never forget our own beauty.

I can feel MM beside me having head-thumping thoughts. She is getting up to walk again. I wish she wouldn't walk so fast sometimes. She doesn't realize she's only following in the footsteps of her own destiny, which will happen no matter how fast she walks. The future will always be there, so why hurry it? Neither of us will ever outwalk the future.

How did she walk with those thoughts for ten hours a day for thirty days when she walked across Spain? She must have had a terrible headache from all those questions. I think her brain has a mind of its own.

My MM and her friends talk about war and terrorism a lot these days. They seem frightened and don't know what to do with their futures. I'm watching to see if the fear I see in their hearts will go away. Will they realize that their fear is of their own making? I watch my MM's every movement. I sit up very straight when I watch her because I want her to know that I'm aware of everything she does, and thinks, and feels.

I'm watching her closely now as we walk each step on the ranch. It's so still around us as a butterfly flutters around my head. I'm looking up to the sky again because I see long jet streams and hear strange sounds way up there. I see my MM looking up too. It feels like she's praying. I can feel her heart go into some kind of reverie that asks for help to make the world more peaceful. Everything around us is so peaceful, but I do understand what she's concerned about.

Shirley

Are we humans about to commence the onslaught fore-
told by the ancient prophecy? Are we seeing pieces fall
into place for the end of the world as we know it? Whatever I turn to—whether it's Revelations in the New Tes-
tament or Nostradamus's predictions, or Hopi and Mayan
prophecies, or Edgar Cayce's channelings, or the Bible—
I see signs that we are on the cusp of a new and devastat-
ing reality that could mean a new, less pleasant, world.

Try as I might, I just can't get the events of the second Gulf War against Iraq out of my mind. I keep thinking back to that time when Ari Fleischer announced that
hostilities were commencing as though he were master of
ceremonies at an execution. I'd been watching the military
buildup all week—our government's warnings and dead-

lines, Baghdad's silence, protests around the world, and emotional farewells as American soldiers were deployed to the Gulf. Were we beginning the third World War?

As a child during World War II, I heard the phrase "theater of war" again and again. Here I was again on opening night, feeling more than ever like a member of the audience in a scripted and directed event. As the several televisions I had going at once blared their messages, I was beside myself with confusion, fear, and rage. Who were we, as humans, much less as Americans, to *initiate* a war? My solar plexus felt tight, leaden, and I couldn't breathe, much less speak with friends who called frantically through the night. I thought of Kurtz in *Apocalypse Now*, "The horror, the horror." I thought of our director, the president, in his many script conferences preparing for *this* performance. I couldn't understand his going through with it in the face of hundreds of thousands of people protesting around the world and in this country. Did he really want so badly to be the hero of his own movie? At his script conferences did anyone ask, What does democracy have to do with killing defenseless people?

On television the show was in full swing, the special effects exploding in the night, buildings falling, palaces burning, like a surreal opera. And somewhere below the fireworks human beings were being burned alive, screaming in despair for themselves and for their children. But I couldn't see them, no Americans could. On that first night, the news reports were all about technologies—precision and accuracy, detailed plans of military strikes and advances. This mayhem was taking place in the cradle of civilization, the birthplace of Abraham, perhaps the very Garden of Eden, where the recorded promise of the human race began. And here we were, bombing it "back to the Stone Age."

Was my beloved country about to unite the Arab world as no Arab leader ever had before? Doing so could only throw gasoline on the fires of a true Holy War. Fundamentalism in any form can look and feel like terrorism to those outside of that faith. Do we really think our own wealth and power come from God? Starting a war is a colossal abuse of privilege, no matter what the justification.

I remember screaming at the television. Terry's ears lay flat against her head as she followed me from room to room. Every now and then she tossed a toy into the air in an unsuccessful attempt to distract me. The talking heads on the screen kept dropping phrases like grenades—September 11, the War on Terror, protecting the homeland—without any real explanation about how these connected to what we were doing: initiating war with a country that had done nothing to provoke us. Our leaders wanted to create a sympathetic audience for this performance, which they told us was about safety and self-preservation in the age of terrorism. But what about *our own* weapons of mass destruction? How could they be justified?

Believe me, doubts about our country's good intentions don't come easily. I am a patriotic American. I was raised in Virginia, home to eight presidents, and growing up I wrote the same thing in my diary every night: "Let the bells ring out in freedom." Our own country was founded by revolutionaries—terrorists to some—who threw off the yoke of British oppression, allowing us in this country the freedom to pursue happiness and to worship in any way we choose. Freedom gave our people prosperity, but far too much of our wealth has been used to create a vast stockpile of technologically precise killing machines to protect that position of privilege. Thinking about it gives me chills.

We have deployed these weapons so that others would live as we saw fit: Let's initiate the violent overthrow of a regime so that government by the people and of the people would thrive. What business was that of ours? Had we not elected our own fair share of thugs in our short history? And what was so democratic about our presidential election in the year 2000, when the popular vote went to a man who would be barred from the presidency?

No one should live under tyranny. Our lives are short and difficult in the best of circumstances, and freedom should be a given. But when we go to war without provocation, I fear that the price of liberating another country may be our souls. Protest is the most patriotic act I can think of, but I don't want my actions to be misunderstood as being unsupportive of the honorable men and women just doing their jobs, following their commander in chief. What *is* his ultimate goal? Is it security, oil, democracy, or just revenge? We still don't have a straight answer.

In the midst of all this, I had to make a decision about whether or not to attend the Academy Awards. It's so strange when the strands of your life become tangled, when politics become personal, even spiritual, and when your profession, already personal, becomes political. I had been invited to Hollywood to be honored as a past Oscar winner. Before the war began I was excited about the prospect. I could catch up on old friends, network for future films, and generally relax and have fun. But as violence in the Gulf escalated, flying to L.A. to parade across the stage in a peach-colored, sequined pantsuit became less and less attractive. I couldn't tolerate the irony of strolling down the red carpet into the Kodak Theater in celebration of ourselves, while our sons and daughters, many of them still teenagers, waited in the wings of another theater wondering if this would be the last day of their lives.

I recall Terry gazing steadily at me as I swung from grief to confusion to fear to rage. Under her patient gaze I sank deeper and deeper into a stony depression, the likes of which I'd never felt before. Finally I climbed into bed, but even with Terry curled up protectively beside me, I couldn't sleep. I needed to get outside, so I sat in the hot tub to try to quiet myself. Night clouds obscured the stars, and I felt a similar haziness inside myself, as though my vision was shrouded by anger and confusion; I prayed for a strong wind to blow through my heart, leaving it empty and clean. I asked for help. I don't know how much time passed when I felt, more than heard, a voice say, "Calm yourself." As if it were an acting exercise, I did. The voice continued, "Your heart is breaking, but it is also opening through the cracks." The clouds began to part, revealing the moon, and the stars shone brighter.

My heart and mind were clearing. I looked out at my mountain that I named Sierra Madre because the old-timers say it is a feminine mountain, inside of which are great treasures. Then a light came from *within* the mountain. The light seemed to glow from below the surface, through the terrain of the slope. I had seen that light before, but couldn't understand where it was coming from. How could light come from *within* a mountain? The phrase "terrain of love" then came to me, followed by the thought, "Nature knows what it is doing even though humankind doesn't." Suddenly I understood with complete certainty that what we had become was due to a profound separation from the Divine Source and we had used our *free will* to do it. From our notion of free will we had created what we call Democracy, a system of government that allowed us to be free to do whatever we wanted as humans—*when* we wanted and *how* we wanted, within certain limits set by laws. But along the way we lost sight of our profound connection to spirit. Because we had been religiously oppressed in Europe before our Revolution, we carried with us the desire to worship in peace. But for most of us, religion promoted divisiveness, not unity: *Our* God was the real God, not theirs. We worshiped God in whatever way we had been taught, but not the Divine way.

This sudden realization that free will could be so dangerous made me wonder if the human race might be a kind of experiment, and that by using free will to sever our connection to the Divine Source, we had set in motion what most prophecies declared as our future. Could two-thirds of the human race be about to destroy itself because of our abuse of our free will?

I looked around me at the peace of the stars. The light from within the mountain disappeared. Was some-one observing me? Were there beings out there, forbid-den to interfere with our impending destruction? Were the shadowed trees and the night birds and Terry herself waiting patiently for us to understand? I sank deeper into the peace I had found and asked for help. The help was there. The inner peace was there. It was a miracle. I was observing it even as I *became* it. It was like allowing a character to inhabit me, instead of the other way around.

Were there other planets whose inhabitants experienced destruction due to their own free will? Was this the mystery of life and the universe? Were the so-called dark forces simply beings who had forgotten their connection to the Divine? And had those dark forces invaded us because we were open to them?

As I sat in the water under the watchful stars, I wondered again if it was too late for us humans. Would the prophecies be fulfilled after all? Gazing up at the night sky it occurred to me that it is in the spaces between things that the truth lies. And the only way to reach it is through calmness, and a faith that it does indeed exist.

Jerry

I don't understand why human beings fight and kill each other so much. It's stupid, because they don't die anyway. They're just making things worse for themselves the next time around.

Sometimes I think people never got past being apes, but then apes don't kill each other nearly so much as people do. Why don't people behave like angels, since that's what they could be? In fact, that's what they are. There is always a way for angels to work out their differences because they know that each of them is part of God. Even the angels they disagree with, or are afraid of, are part of God. When my MM was a little girl she asked her father why there couldn't be peace in the world. He sighed and said, "Because religion makes too many people kill each other."

Shirley

I came to realize how deeply rooted belief in the Devil is in our culture, and how it can be applied to suit the human powers that be, during my preparation to play the character Rebecca Nurse in *The Witches of Salem* television miniseries. It's more than mere coincidence that the witches of Salem also happened to be women who inherited or owned property themselves in a male-dominated society.

Rebecca Nurse was one of the most pious women in the village, attending and cleaning the church every day, but her belief in a loving God was more important to her than her fear of the Devil. Her hanging marked the end of the witch trials, although she was pardoned for her crimes only a few years ago.

The day we shot the hanging scene I took Terry to the outdoor location, framed by a misty, eerie sky. I had been hoisted onto a cart with a rope around my neck. Terry sat some distance from the cart with my friend and assistant. The director yelled "Action!" through a bull-horn, and all of the villagers, children, and adults began to wail, and moan, and cry. Terry's ears went back and she began to bark and howl as she ran over to my cart and tried to climb up. As the wailing grew louder, Terry grew extremely alarmed. She couldn't understand that this wasn't real. Someone pushed her away, and finally she fled. My assistant found her, but she wouldn't come back to the set. Terry felt the emotional "reality" that we actors created, and was not happy with how we manipulated our personalities in order to play the scene. I realized yet again how disturbing creating our reality can be—in "reel" life as well as "real" life!

Terry

When my MM took me to the set where she was about to
be hung I had a sense that she and the other actors were
going to play a trick on their feelings—and that I might
be very confused. But I didn't realize how awful it would
be. I saw small children and grown-ups who should have
known better, acting as though they were afraid of what
they called the Devil.

At first MM was dressed in her Pilgrim clothes, and
she threw a stick for me to chase, which I did but I knew
something bad was going to happen. Everyone seemed
normal until a big man shouted "Action!" and everyone
began to make sad noises. I didn't know what was wrong.
What had just changed?

My MM, in the cart with a rope around her neck,

looked up at the sky and started to pray. I had seen her do it at the ranch, but this time it scared me so I tried to jump into the cart to save her. When someone pushed me away I thought I had done something wrong because everyone was acting so upset. So I ran away. MM's friend took me back to her trailer, but I could still hear everyone moaning in the distance. It was truly a terrible experience for me. If that is what they call acting, then I'm wondering what I can depend on when it comes to sincerity with human beings. Maybe they act a little bit all the time. I never act unless it's important, or a matter of survival.

When MM finally came back to me in her trailer, I didn't know what to expect. She hadn't been herself only a little while before. Or had she? How do these actor people do all that without touching some part of themselves that is real? I don't know what they think real is. Acting is a mystery to me.

My MM knelt down and told me she was very sorry, and that I hadn't done anything wrong. That made me feel better, but I wanted to talk to her about this Devil business.

Did those hangings really happen to those women, just because other people said they were supposedly friendly with the Devil? Who was this Devil anyway? I know what humans think about evil, but who is this person who puts a "d" in front of that word? Is it important that "evil" is "live" spelled backward? Humans certainly have a backward approach to living. When will they see the Light?

Shirley

Even though I'm questioning whether to make the movie in Ireland, and even though I'm questioning the role of movies themselves in our society (particularly given what is being made), I know in my heart that good films probably have a more profound effect on human lives than anything other than war. This may be why audiences are so drawn to violence. Perhaps they need to examine the violence in themselves. We never made much "violence" in the old days, when movies were more about the relationships people had with each other. I suppose the reflected violence of what we've become has its place.

Sometimes on a film set now I feel I represent a more chivalrous time. When I work on a picture these days I'm referred to as "ma'am" instead of "kid" or "girl." And there usually comes a moment when I'm surrounded by younger artists and crew members asking what it was like to work with Alfred Hitchcock, Sam Goldwyn, Harry Cohen, Mike Todd, Jack Lemmon, Robert Mitchum, William Wyler, Billy Wilder, and the rest of the greats. They were artists who yearned to reflect the *power* of the human spirit in their desire to entertain, not the *loss* of the human spirit. Artists in my day didn't care that much about fashion, tabloids, or even grosses.

I realize that I absorbed something in all those years working with those purveyors of inspiring film images, something that many young artists today don't seem to appreciate: all of the old timers had a strong work ethic, which came out of a deep belief in what they were doing. Lots of people in the business today don't seem to have the personal training, or the deep-seated need to express that which we are missing in our lives.

I've found that the discipline I learned from dancing also keeps me healthy and balanced under the considerable stress of making a movie, and in the constant prying glare of the public eye. When I was working on a TV miniseries about Mary Kay, the queen of door-to-door cosmetic sales, I noticed that we were way behind schedule, with only one day left to get three days of work done. To catch up we had to work straight through from 8:30 Thursday morning to 1:30 Friday afternoon. One scene we had to run through at least a dozen times involved me walking up and down stairs. I think the cast expected me to collapse, or at least to lose my balance or my temper, but those years of discipline stood me in good stead. The work ethic and heart balance you learn when you're young stay with you forever.

If your desire is to be a long distance runner, the industry that makes art out of illusion requires stamina of the heart, mind, and body. Too many young artists today care more about popularity with the public than about what they wish to express. The public is leading them rather than the other way around. Just as importantly, I've learned that filming is not about the individual; it's a team experience as well as an endurance sport.

And more than anything it is a spiritual exercise. Scratch the skin of any artist and you'll find a spiritual seeker; when artists resonate to that aspect of themselves they do their best work, in my opinion.

One of the great pleasures I take in later years is being cantankerous about professionalism. Now people expect me to insist that a profound work ethic be observed, and to not care what anybody thinks of that. If I'm not eccentric, hard-driving, and insistent on everyone pulling their weight, people are actually disappointed! I find that aging goes better if you're a little loony anyhow. Particularly if your coworkers think you talk to God!

Terry

*My MM is seeing that nature itself is very efficient. Nothing is gratuitous or unimportant. It is a lot like that making **good** movies, from what I've seen. Every living being has a part to play and a job to do, which ultimately results in a harmonious message. But neither nature nor moviemaking is a democracy. The ultimate authority in nature is the Divine. The ultimate authority in a movie is the director. The Divine has a vision just as the director does, and those who defy either authority are in for a tough time. The Divine and the director may listen democratically to suggestions, but in the end I've noticed that with each it will go the way of the master. Humans don't listen to the divine director in nature and many of them give the movie* *director a hard time too. As I've observed, moviemaking can be a divine experience, but if people don't listen and support the vision of the one upstairs, whether on the set or in heaven, they should go make their own movie.*

Shirley

I sometimes take Terry with me to movie business meetings because she changes the environment so dramatically. Everyone starts off thinking the meeting is going to be about money and schedules and things of that sort. But Terry completely disarms everybody the moment she walks in. We all have a natural desire to be a child, and that's what Terry brings out in people. Children don't care about money or schedules. People are confused when they see I've brought my dog, but after a few minutes they understand there's some sort of wisdom in it, and within fifteen or twenty minutes with Terry, they've touched that wisdom in themselves.

I particularly like taking Terry to a script conference because the director, the producer, and the actors are all playing parts even before the production begins. Terry seems to understand that there are many characters involved in the room. I love to see how she reacts to hard-bitten producers who don't like anyone to see the childlike part of themselves. They're always the ones whose laps she decides to jump up on. That alters the producer's desire to save money in favor of allowing the artistic vision to prevail, even if it costs more.

Taking Terry shopping has a profound effect too, because when people see a friendly little animal jump up on them, it seems to absolve them of the guilt of spending money they secretly think they shouldn't be spending. This is true for me, as well. In a dressing room Terry observes everything I put on. If she jumps up on me, that's the outfit I buy. In a pet store if she sees a toy she wants she sits in front of it and stares it down. Her silent language communicates to me—and she always gets what she wants.

New York can be a cool experience, because everyone seems to be into themselves, rushing to their next appointment and projecting autonomy in their universe, as if to protect themselves from the knowledge of their own vulnerability. Although it takes a little bit longer for a New Yorker to let his or her façade crack when Terry jumps up, it always happens. And when I go to places in New York where there are many famous people and photographers lurking around, I notice how the level of competitive energy drops when Terry walks in. (The stars may also be aware of W. C. Fields's famous advice not to be photographed with dogs or children!)

Terry

Competition can pit people against one another in a destructive way. What they need to realize is that they should be in competition with themselves to be more trusting.

One time we were in New York, and my MM was having a meeting with a very temperamental writer. She asked him to make some changes in a scene. He began to argue with MM only because he thought his territory was being invaded. I know something about that so I jumped on his lap. He was surprised, but then he began to pet me, and MM got what she wanted. She and I make a good artistic team, because life is an art.

Maybe we should have dogs accompany their masters at the UN. I could wear a doggie burka. When the people argue, and call each other monkeys, we could bark.

When they call each other worse names that make them even madder, we could jump on their laps and tug at their beards. Then we would nip their noses until they agreed to respect each other, which really means they are respecting themselves.

Shirley

A dark cloud of concern comes over me because I really don't want to go to Ireland and leave Terry. It's beginning to obsess me. Is making a good movie my top priority? That was my *modus operandi* most of my life. What I really should be doing is making a movie about what I'm learning. But what would be the plot? Where would the dramatic tension come from? Not many people watched *The Witches of Salem,* which I thought revealed an important aspect of where we Americans came from spiritually—our history of seeing the Devil in other people.

The sun comes out, and then slips behind a bank of dark clouds. In the distance we hear the low roll of thunder. The weather here is moody, just like me. Is it reflecting me? Terry and I are walking the land and I'm thinking that being a "senior citizen" has its advantages and disadvantages. I know that growing old is not for sissies, and hiking works much the same way, but I'm feeling that the wisdom I've accumulated and the sense of a bit more peace within me was well worth the wait. Still, I want more. I'm glad that I will never be young again, at least not this time around. I'm more interested in a partnership with my body now, not the kind of adversarial relationship I had with it when I was young and a dancer.

Traveling in Argentina once, I saw an advertisement for cheap tickets to a vaudeville show with the great Maya Plisetskaya on the bill. I couldn't believe it was *the* Maya Plisetskaya, one of the finest ballerinas of all time, dancing at her age—middle sixties—and for a pittance. I had seen her perform at the Bolshoi in Russia on many occasions, and when the Bolshoi started coming to the States I got to know her well. During the Cold War I had a party for her and the Bolshoi at my home. It was a time when Americans presumed that wholesale repression existed throughout Soviet society, but even with the KGB in attendance there was a degree of uninhibited sensual behavior most Americans wouldn't have indulged in, even in private. At two in the morning I poured Galliano for the troupe of Russian dancers and they slowly dispersed throughout the grounds, disappearing behind flowering bushes and trees, doing, I suppose, what dancers all over the world do with enough Galliano in their systems. Even some KGB officers found their way into that sylvan wood, taking an altogether different kind of attendance!

Curious, I bought a ticket to the show in Argentina. Would Maya Plisetskaya really dance again? She came out in the middle of the show dressed in her famous swan costume. She had set the standard for this role, and at sixty-five she could still perform the pas de bourees and elegantly, disintegrating, gestures of the dying swan. Still, I couldn't help thinking how humiliating it was that Plisetskaya had to dance on a vaudeville stage in South America to make ends meet. When she got a standing ovation and returned for an encore, I was struck by the poignancy of her dancing the dying swan in the later years of her life. Margot Fonteyn told me once, "When we're old enough as dancers to know what we're doing and how to act through the movement, we're too old to dance."

Plisetskaya as the dying swan has stayed with me as an image of how we drag the past into the present. I can no longer dance before an audience in a way that would be acceptable to me, but acting is different. I feel like the canvas of my understanding and experience gets painted with richer hues as I age, and I am more capable than ever of expressing a broad, complex range of emotions. I may worry sometimes about how I look onstage or before the camera, but as we older actresses know, the secret to looking good is expert lighting.

The sun is shining on my face now, and its light is merciless. I wish I had a good key light or a bigger hat. These hills are steep and I'm out of breath, but as Art Linkletter once said, "It's better to be over the hill than under it."

Terry

As my Mistress Mother examines her life I can feel her wondering if her days of self-expression are over. They are not. With age she will find there is more to express than ever. I want her to express until she no longer has the energy to stop! And what she expresses will be more important if I have anything to say about it.

Memory is getting to be an issue for my MM. I see her with friends who are her own age, and some who are twenty years younger, forgetting things all the time. They can't remember the phone number of a good friend. They can't even remember the name of the friend sometimes. They can't remember where they put their car keys, and when they do finally find them, sometimes they can't remember what they're for! So I'm very aware that my Mis-

tress Mom feels frustrated by her memory loss, but I know she's really going through a kind of elevation of understanding, focusing on important things beyond the details.

I don't like to see my MM irritated when her memory fails her, because I know that with my help she is slowly entering these other dimensions that I am tuned in to. Sometimes, when she has forgotten what it is she was supposed to do, she says things to herself like, "I don't know what is happening to my mind." At times like that I always go over to her and put my head in her lap until she strokes me. I tell her to let her memory rest in peace, then she relaxes and picks me up, so I think she gets the message. Speaking of the importance of messages, I have told her, and she understands, that she should not lift me up under my front legs because that's hard on my shoulders. What she does now, thank goodness, is put both of her hands on my tummy. When she lifts me up that way it's much more comfortable, and I think everybody should know that about us fur persons.

Shirley

Terry is attempting to dig into an anthill. I am concerned, so I say "NO, Terry, NO." She stops digging and
looks up at me. Sometimes the word "no" is too painful
for me to utter because Terry's ears go flat with fear. Or
is it shame? Perhaps she is just disappointed that I can't
find a more positive way to say what's on my mind.

Terry

I don't perceive "no" as an attack. I cower because my MM is afraid for me unnecessarily, and she scares me when she's afraid of something. I like to please her but not by being afraid like she is. There's nothing to be afraid of in an anthill. Ants are beings too, and they know I'm doing my job as a dog.

The animal, insect, and plant kingdoms are so much more in touch with the spiritual essence of God than humans are. I know because we silently communicate with each other on this subject. God is in everything we see, so God is in the anthill. The ants themselves have knowledge of spirit that lies beyond the human power of reasoning. I wish MM would understand this. I see my MM's "no" as a problem she's having with her own fear because she has forgotten that the ants are part of God. It's true that her fear is something she has created in herself, not something that is real. And out of that perception comes the need to control, and defend, and ultimately, "NO!"

My MM is always looking around and asking herself, "What is the meaning of all this?" But when she sees this little dog digging in an anthill, who doesn't seem to have a purpose except to just dig, she wonders why she needs to know what anything is for. I am all being, and no "I am." I have no ego. It is her ego that drives her toward ambition, success, or failure, toward goals that are always just beyond reach. Life is what happens between activities. The path is the goal. If she just loves what she's doing, then her goal won't be all that interesting or important to her.

We pets have become so much a part of the human family because we greet humans again and again with the joy that is missing in their own lives. We help them realize that their only purpose here is to be happy. That's what God wishes for us. That's what She sees when she looks into my soulful eyes. Yet they aren't taught happiness, even in childhood, and certainly not in school. The first lessons for their children and their pets are "No, you can't do this, and you can't do that," even though what they treasure in us is our residence in a reality unbounded by time or fear or judgment.

Regardless of how well or badly they treat us, we pets will still greet them with unconditional love the next time they see us. That is what they could have for themselves. A friend of MM's once said, "I would much rather come home to my dog than to a person, because my dog won't tell me how I've screwed up his life." That's what we're here for.

MM and I can take the same walk every day, and for me it is a thrilling adventure every time. Humans are tethered to the past and fearful of the future, so they usually end up dragging themselves through the present. I am the creator of the world I want to see; I am inventing the world in every moment. I live completely in the present, which is why I can jump on MM with joy fifteen minutes after she has reprimanded me for digging into an anthill. That doesn't mean I'm forgetful; it means I'm free.

*This is the way God intends for **people** to live. I know that MM feels I am holy to her. And when I am around her, **she** feels holy. I have "issues" in my own life, but I never stray from my spiritual essence. I remain part of the "is-ness." I know I bring joy to most everyone who sees me on the beach, on the street, in a taxi, or in an elevator in New York; I know I bring joy to everyone who encounters me on our ranch—even the ants. Because of that joy my MM feels that the very rug I sleep on or the very chair I sit on becomes a holy relic to her. I'm not being arrogant. I want my MM to feel my energy after I leave it. I want her next to me so that my little body can infuse her with my spirit.*

When I do something that displeases MM, I don't feel guilty. Guilt is a kind of living hell. Guilt is based on a feeling of having sinned, but what is sin? There is no such thing as sin. We are all part of God, and how can God sin? God is perfect. God is love. People's perception that they have sinned is an illusion they have created because they feel separate from God. Only if they are sep-

*arate from God could they sin. But **other than God
doesn't exist**. And if God is all that exists, then sin cannot
exist. Sinlessness is a promise from God that we are made
of love and light.*

*If people are truly in touch with the God in them-
selves, then God speaks to them all through the day. This is
what MM sees in me. God's spirit speaks to me and sus-
tains me. Yes, MM always wants to be with me because
something tells her that she is lonely for the God in herself. When she is upset with things, when the world seems
to impose itself on her, I am with her. I feel her turmoil
and sometimes it throws me out of balance, but then I tell
her that she is upset because she's out of touch with something really simple—the reality that God **is** everything,
which she has replaced with the illusion of being upset. I
say to her, "You are really upset by nothing. Why don't
you understand that?"*

*Nothing needs to be done, because everything already
is. Then MM asks, if that is so, how does one live that way?
I watch her go through a moment of doubt, anger, or pain. I*

just watch. And when I feel the moment is right, I come over and put my paws on her knees or I take a flying leap across the room and jump into her arms, as though to reassure her I am real, not one of her uncomfortable illusions. When she looks into my eyes and I lick her face, I'm saying, "Your own best interest is to know that you can simply trust. I trust you, why don't you trust you?"

MM looks to God above.
She should look down at me.
I'm the ONE who knows.

Statue of Anubis.

Yes, I am Anubis.

"Oh Wise One of Ancient Knowledge," MM says to me.

This is an air pirouette.

See my incredible chest capacity? I lift weights.

I'm waiting for a vicious German Shepherd.

This is called a Grand Jeté in ballet terms.

This is called "chase the seagull" in beach language.

This is called "down dog" pose in Ashanga yoga.

MM thinks I can't climb up the steps myself. How foolish ...

MM's boobies are not too high for me.

I'm even in command of the sun.

My future is secure.

We're dreaming about long ago.

I like to look taller and longer whenever possible.

My throne under the tree of knowledge of good and evil.

I'm gazing into the past.

I am an expert driver.

I like to make MM
think I'm begging.

Do I get a dessert later?

Sheba is a magnificent but older female.

But Daisy is a sweet older woman.

Daisy is waiting for me to come out and order her around.

Daisy and
Sandy "kiss
talking."

One blue eye,
one dark eye and
still Spooky waits
to seduce me.

They all
succumb
to my orders.

My MM is going to dunk
her face in the stream.

Domestic bliss.

Shirley

I see a light in Terry's dark eyes now. In that light is profundity, patience, timelessness, fearlessness, and quiet strength. She embodies the paradox that by being totally vulnerable, totally trusting, she can never truly be harmed. When she looks into my eyes, it is as though Terry is forgiving me for not forgiving myself, while at the same time reminding me that forgiveness isn't even necessary. No, I certainly don't want to travel and leave her behind.

Jerry

Why does my MM have to achieve something in order to be happy? She knows there are no goals, but then she will say, "Well, what about work?" "What about my need to relate to other people?" And "What about my self-esteem if I don't do something well enough?" I say, "Look at me, I don't have to achieve anything and I don't hold griev- ances about what you might scold me for. I'm always in touch with the light inside myself. Holding on to worries just blocks your view of the light inside of you. And the person you hold the grievance for is an illusion you've cre- ated anyway. Why don't you give up both?"

As I look up at the southwestern sky. I see a faraway object that is round and brightly lit. It begins to zip in and out of the clouds as it gets closer. I know what it is. It's one of our star people friends. Humans see them too, because I've heard people tell stories of seeing flying craft of some kind, that appear in and around the mountains here.

One guest at the ranch said he was sitting in MM's hot tub at sunset when he saw three round objects come out of her mountain and literally hang in the air, way above his head. He said he couldn't believe what he was seeing. He said he smelled roses and felt something "trying to touch my mind." After floating in the air for a few minutes the aircraft rose straight up and disappeared back into the mountain. He told MM he felt a strong spiritual energy and he noticed that soon after that his life changed. He became clearer about what he was doing and much happier. He met and fell in love with someone special. He said his life had become a dream. Well, life is a dream. And people can make it anything they want. They have that kind of power, they just don't realize it. We animals do this all the time when the humans don't interfere.

Once a very old dog friend of mine who could barely hobble around on his unsteady arthritic legs decided it was time to pass on, and disappeared into the woods during a family outing. His master called him back, and he obeyed. The dog silently talked with the family about all the good times they had shared, and when he walked unsteadily back into the woods, the family knew they would never see him again. But one day, after he had passed over, he observed his family out on another walk together. He decided to become a dream dog and ran toward them really fast. He acknowledged his beloved family but never stopped to let them reach out and pet him. Yet they knew he had come back to say he was happy in his new life, and that now he could run as fast as he wanted to.

Many of my friends who have passed on come to their human companions in dreams. They press their furry selves against their human friends with all the warmth they can muster; they nudge and paw until their masters wake up. They do it to remind their human loved ones that nothing ever dies. Love just changes form.

I knew a little three-year-old boy once who loved the dog next door. One night the dog died in his sleep, and the boy woke up screaming, "Doggie died, doggie died!" As you see, we communicate with young people better than adult people.

Many of us wake our MMs to warn them of impending danger, like a fire or a burst pipe, or an intruder or something like that. I haven't yet had to do that. But I certainly would if it were necessary.

Shirley

Terry and I stand in a dreamlike state. I have just seen a flying object in the sky. It was brightly lit and hovered over us until it disappeared right into the side of Sierra Madre Mountain. This is not the first time I have seen it, but every time it has the power to shock me into silence. What is it? I think Terry saw it too. I notice that the trees are still. The pond is still. The clouds are still. All the animals are still too, perfectly in touch with that still point I long to touch in myself. A gentle wind begins to blow through the stillness, and a light cleansing rain begins to fall. Then a slight cold chill shivers through me. The stillness seems to adjust to the chill. Is this what they call the chill of Truth? I try to understand, but I can't. I am not fully in touch with the rhythms of nature—and with whatever has just happened.

This being a holiday weekend, the other people who work here on the ranch are gone. I see Terry and her brother and sister animals on the ranch looking into the sky. Did they intuit that something "out of this world" just happened? What are they feeling? What is coursing through their minds and spirits? Do they feel an alien consciousness calling them? What communications are they picking up? Do they wish to educate me? The dogs raise their heads further and sniff the air. Then they sigh. It's as if they've been told that peace is possible. Do these craft have occupants, and if so are they children of God? Are they ever afraid? Where did fear come from, anyway? How did we get to be "God-fearing" people? What does that mean? That we must fear the very thing that created us? When we are still, and far away from the many distractions of our "civilized" world, we can hear the truth. How can love be feared then? Have we chosen to believe that God is to be feared because we fear the love we are capable of in ourselves? Are we uncomfortable with its quiet power, its still certitude?

Terry

I like standing here with a stick in my mouth, not knowing why I picked it up, or what I'm going to do with it. I like just standing here. If I sense a craft overhead, it doesn't bother me. I know what it is. I've seen lots of them. I am perfectly happy with this stick in my mouth, doing nothing. In another minute I may start to chew on it, but if I do the stick will be perfectly fine with my need to chew it. It isn't afraid of me. I know it isn't afraid of me because I can feel its energy, and its energy doesn't know anything about fear. Everything and everyone is energy. So why should anything be afraid? We should just be attentive.

My MM watches me carry the stick under a tree that gives me shade on this sunny, magical Easter weekend. She's looking around because she doesn't know what to think about anything. I wish she'd just play with me, but my MM is too busy thinking and wondering.

I know that to her our animal play looks like fighting sometimes, but we know the difference through the sound of our growls, and we make sure to bite each other on the neck, where loose skin and lots of fur make it safe. Yes, we have a pecking order, and yes, we have squabbles, but we settle them without killing. When we fight to establish dominance or chase off another male trying for our female's attention, we don't fight to the death, we just fight until one dog turns over and exposes his throat. We have no equivalent to the war that my MM worries about. So what is war to us dogs? It's stupid and it kills living beings. We don't like that at all because if it goes too far we won't have anyone to play with.

Shirley

As I stand looking out at God's country, I try to remember a time when I was perfectly at peace. There are not many moments when I seemed to disappear into what I saw, when I had no concerns, no thought of the past or future, when I was only aware of now. Once as a child I was walking past a garden of colorful pansies when suddenly I seemed to become the pansies, with their color, their scent, and their essence. In those moments I found total bliss, and I've never forgotten it. I see Terry doing this all day long. Right now she's sticking her little nose into a desert flower and breathing in the white of it. In a while she will nibble on the herbs in my garden.

When we speak of our pets giving us love, what do we mean? Are they always in a spiritual state, a state beyond judgment?

I have a friend whose son was murdered. She not only forgave the murderer, but she became his keeper. When he was released from prison, she took responsibility for him and brought him into her own home. Knowing that she and I both shared a belief in the law of karma, the Buddhist principle of cause and effect, I asked her, "Do you believe that on some level you played a part in the death of your son?" It was very hard for her to admit, and almost as hard for me to hear, but she said, yes, the lesson learned from the death of her son was something she needed in order to learn forgiveness. Our own karma always plays a role.

My friend had cut herself off from God before her son was murdered. Then she reconnected to Spirit, and all of the laws of cause and effect in her life became clear. She knew that what we put out returns to us. She said it was not a punitive concept, but a law of nature, the Law of One. Because of her experience, and the understanding she gained from it, my friend became a beacon of hope and insight for others. She is peaceful and happy despite the terrible tragedy she suffered.

I look at Terry and wonder if my love for her is some sort of overcompensation for not having been there for my own daughter. Is Terry my new daughter? Could I have taken more pleasure in the rearing of my own child if I had realized sooner what I know now? Perhaps. I didn't know how to be present with myself then, let alone with someone else.

It seems almost ridiculous to say it, but a dog is so much easier to raise, in part because I accept that her identity has nothing to do with me. It doesn't require me to do anything right. Terry is so obviously and completely herself. She barks, she licks, she plays, and she loves. It's that simple, and it's that foolproof. Although her identity is infinite, she is teaching me that now is everything. With children we constantly worry about the future.

So I look at my peaceful, meaningful landscape and I try to figure out how to be a part of the other, "real," world. Knowing it's an illusion, why do I want to go back into it? It all seems so crazy to me right now. Is that just because of the way I perceive it? If so, then to change the world I have to change my own perceptions. I don't want to live in a world that is enslaved by ambition, by technology, by power, by terror, by competition, by anxiety, and greed. I don't want to give those dark forces substance by thinking they're real. In little ways I've seen the world around me change by the way I perceive it. Could it possibly be that there is no world at all outside of our collective and individual dream?

When my mother was dying she saw all the people in the world as hearts beating in unison, connected to each other by a golden thread. Right before her passing, she said she wished that we could see that thread connecting us all, because if we could, we would never be unhappy again. That moment reminded me of a vision she had had years before, when she saw that trees and the earth and even people were filled with inner light, and there was a gentle wind moving within that light. She said there was also light *within* the earth, radiating up and out to those of us who walked upon it.

For all her amazing visions, as she approached the time of her passing, my mother told the doctors she could no longer see. After a full battery of tests, the doctors could find no physical reason for it. I think she just didn't want to see anything beyond her inner vision any more. She wanted to be free of life's conflicts. Making decisions had always been difficult for my mother, but at the end everything was simple. There were no complications, just love. Sometimes she only wanted her cat, Gypsy, in the room with her. I think the aloof mysteriousness of that cat was a comfort to my mother as she prepared to enter the great mystery herself, especially by contrast to our hovering, worried family love.

My father's transition was longer. Each day my father would tell his nurses and doctors about his spirit travels the night before, when he visited his father, his mother, and his other relatives that had crossed over. They told him things. They told him about his life before he was born, and about the history of the Earth and the human race. Every morning doctors and nurses at Johns Hopkins would come by for an informal seminar at the foot of my father's bed. It was remarkable because these were conventional medical doctors, yet they all seemed to understand that when someone is in the process of passing, they gain access to privileged information and higher knowledge.

One of the finest surgeons at Johns Hopkins told me later that often when he was operating he felt guided, as if his hands were being held and moved by an invisible master. He said he had learned to let go and trust this force to direct his movements, and in doing so had become uncommonly skilled, saving hundreds of lives.

Jerry

There are many angels guiding the human race but they are having a difficult time because the humans don't think it's possible. It doesn't matter though, because everything is happening just as it should. It was determined a long time ago. I just wish people would be more open to the guidance. Then they wouldn't suffer so much. What the people in the world have created is insane. What I am living is sane. I rest in spirit so I am balanced. I close my eyes and I sink into a stillness that is perfect.

Shirley

The rains have passed and the dogs and I are setting out for a walk along a path which will be peppered with piñon and juniper trees. Once this was the land of towering ponderosa pines and tall grasses, until the white man leveled the trees and turned his cattle and sheep loose to graze. Millions of years before that, this was a vast savannah where dinosaurs roamed. I sometimes wonder if their spirits are still here, bearing silent witness to the endless flow of change. If so, they will make themselves known to Spooky, my alpha spirit dog, who, as always, is in the lead.

I move with Terry, Sheba, and the rest of the pack, and the sun is part of me. When the dogs are at my side I am more alert to the world around me. I take notice of a spring blossom that has come out overnight, and I imagine the snows from the higher mountains melting to create the stream that runs alongside us. I lie face-down in the stream with my clothes on, remembering that this water purifies itself every hundred yards. The dogs stand quietly watching me. I am part of their pack yet their leader. They don't wade in splashing or barking or shaking themselves in delight. It's as if they know I don't want the water muddied, that I am savoring its purity. I'm different from them yet one of them.

It's difficult to explain the freedom I feel as I drink the icy water flowing under my nose and mouth. I am primitive, availing myself of the sacred gifts of nature.

Terry

While MM had her face in the stream I saw two rabbits chasing each other. Then they stopped and one got on top of the other. At first I didn't know what they were doing. Then I walked away to give them some privacy, which I thought they would enjoy, but I really wanted to go back and ask them some questions about rabbit sex. I see that human sex certainly has a lot of people confused!

I think people make too much of sex. It's certainly not an issue for me, since I've been neutered, and it's not much of an issue for MM, who went through menopause some time ago. I do wonder why people let sex run so much of their lives. Sex is something to be enjoyed when everything else works.

Sex for its own sake was never that interesting to MM, even though it is for lots of humans. Emotional inti-

155

*macy was always what made sex fun for MM, and inti-
macy is all about trust. Looking down on her life I saw
that when she was younger, sex certainly had more inten-
sity because her hormones were raging, but as she got older
her hormones stopped running her love life. And what a
relief it is for her to be free of that.*

*Now MM finds a man "erotic" who reveals his vul-
nerabilities and values to the world. I, of course, don't find
it erotic, but I like men who act like that. Human attraction
is often a matter of art, I think, and since so many people
are artists I wonder how they can be faithful to one partner
for a lifetime. Why does this society feel that "monogamy"
is necessary? If a partner is a possession that might make
sense, but owning someone never really seems to work.*

*When MM talks to me about sex I tell her I would
be turned on by someone who likes to play. She likes that
too. She is also turned on by mischief, as am I. Cuddling is
good too—feeling deep contentment curling up with someone who truly understands you is something we both love.
Happily, we give that to each other.*

Sometimes when we're channel surfing we will come across a show on television with naked people having sex, and we always get bored by all the grunting and moaning. Maybe it's because we know they're acting. Maybe MM acted a little bit in such moments too, thinking sex required a performance from her, but she doesn't feel that way anymore, to my great relief. Performance was certainly never an issue for me. In fact, in this lifetime I've never experienced sex, and I couldn't care less.

Sometimes my MM feels guilty about having had me neutered because she'd love to know what my babies would be like. But she's really my child, as anyone can see. When I first met Spooky, the alpha male, he tried to make me his Barbie possession by peeing on me to stake out his turf. That was not smart. I tolerated this for a while, and then one day I flirted with him until he rolled over on his back. Then I straddled him, squatted, and peed on his face! He never approached me again.

I flirt with everybody really. I do it by jumping up on them and nipping their noses. If humans flirt with each other and it leads to something more I don't see anything wrong with it. Neither does God. In fact, God likes people to enjoy each other's bodies, as long as they don't hurt each other.

Bodies are wonderfully expressive human machinery. But it's a waste of machinery if they only use them to make babies. There are too many babies in the world anyway. I enjoy looking at human bodies. They are so beautiful, and sometimes funny, and really nice to cuddle up to. Those times when I see people on TV with no clothes on their bodies doing their sex stuff, they do it too fast. They go so fast when they move together that I don't know how they can enjoy their beautiful machinery. They should slow down. We were much slower in Egypt when we built all those majestic monuments. People and gods were living up to the bigness of their spirits back then.

But now humans are delusional. They think they have to be thin to be attractive, yet that must feel very bony in bed. They are obsessed with not being fat. They should be healthy, of course, but that's more about loving themselves than it is about what other people think. Humans seem to care an awful lot about "keeping up with the Bone-ses," and with buying expensive clothes at discount prices.

People have such strange ideas about what's attractive. They don't seem to go for the heart as much as they go for the "sexy" body. And of course they don't really know how to play. If they ever have a problem they should just roll over on their back. People haven't learned to roll over yet. They keep on arguing. Exposed tummies are very good problem solvers, and thankfully I have been seeing more of those lately.

One thing I don't like to see is male humans in middle age going for younger women just to prove that they can still perform in bed. What is this performance business? Why don't they just enjoy themselves? And the younger women seem to go for those older men because they have money. To me they are both ridiculous. And the funny thing about it is that everyone else knows what's really going on.

As for MM and me, we don't have much time for sex anyway. If it came along, fine, but I think we'd rather be in bed with each other. There are fewer problem—no backtalk, no orders—and we can live our lives the way we want to.

We are both more interested in, shall we say, social inter-course. What interests us is how people walk, talk, think, play, and how much of themselves they are willing to share.

I'm watching humans as they grapple with the sub-ject of what they call "gay" sex. I don't understand the problem. Neither does God. America's president recently said, "We are all sinners." Well, he couldn't be more wrong. He just thinks that people are sinners, which of course leads to all kinds of problems. Souls live in bodies, and every soul has its own taste.

It's fun for me to see a hu-man man dressed up like a woman, because that means he enjoys looking good, just like my MM. What people do with their bodies is their business. I think most people get their opinions about sex from religion. It seems like very religious people don't usu-ally have a very free attitude about sex. I think it may have to do with their confusion about whether God or Jesus or Mary had sex.

I think religion confuses people about many things. It can make them afraid of God, of each other, and even of

*dying, since the Bible says that they're not coming around
again, except for Jesus on Easter, and the Second Coming.
But there are other good books that say they are. I think it
would be better if people were taught that they were going
to be reborn—then they'd realize they couldn't get away
with anything because they'd just carry that old baggage
into their new life. They'd realize they might as well take
responsibility now and get it over with.*

*I hear my MM and her friends having long talks
about the difference between religion and what they call
spirituality. I'd like to say a few things about that too. Religion happened a long time ago when people stopped being
able to read each other's thoughts. If you can't read
people's thoughts you have to depend on words, and that
can lead to manipulation, which can lead to religion. For
humans maybe religion began when beings came down
from the sky and were mistaken for God. Maybe the sky
visitors saw that humans were cruel to each other so they
decided to give them rules to establish control. When they
told people all the things they couldn't do instead of all the*

things they were capable of doing, that's how religion was born. Humans became "God-fearing" people, and sex-fearing people, and full-of-guilt people.

In my time in Egypt with MM we had lots of gods. We had gods of thunder and gods of lightning and gods of water and gods of sun and gods of moon and gods of plants and gods of dogs and gods of cats. As Anubis I was one of the most important because I spoke to people about no-death. Maybe we **should** *have lots of gods since everything around us is part of God. Nobody put it all together into one thing called religion back then. But whether it's one god or many, I certainly don't believe it's right to kill people over whoever they think their god is. I don't know any gods who would like that either. When people kill they build up negative karma, regardless of their reasons.*

I know MM thinks religion is a real problem in the world. She's concerned about a holy war. For some humans nothing is more important than their God, so when different fundamentalist groups of people like that decide their God is the **only** *God, things can get very nasty. And nasty karma is not good for anyone.*

Humans should understand that down through time they have each experienced being both male and female. That was the way they learned about each other. But I must say from what I've observed regarding their "war of the sexes," they haven't learned fast enough. Each person should be a reflection of the soul, and each soul is equally balanced between male and female. That has been difficult for humans to understand, which has created a lot of complicated karma relating to the sexes.

All humans have unresolved karma with each other. In fact, the reason they are alive on earth is to clean up their karmic issues. Families can be the most difficult things to sort out because family members have souls that need the most resolution with each other. If they went within themselves and touched their souls' past, the world would be a more peaceful place.

Shirley

I think a lot about the karma I may have with those people dearest to me—mother, father, brother, daughter, lovers, and friends—because my love has always contained an element of judgment. I think I never allowed anyone to be unconditionally themselves. I remember once being deeply in love with a man who told me he never felt that he was living up to my expectations. I felt the same way about him. I feel the same way about my daughter too, and I love her as much as anyone.

Independence has likely always been a karmic sticking point for me too, especially when it comes to romantic love. Most men are protective, which makes me feel more like a possession than an equal partner. With my parents I always felt like a daughter, as opposed to my own person. I was always my father's little girl, even when I was 60. That's not true with an animal, so perhaps we don't have as much karma with them. Animals take us at face value based on who we are right here and now.

My mother was extremely withholding with her emotions. She said it was more diplomatic to be that way. That may be why I'm so direct. My father was not diplomatic. He didn't curb his feelings at all. He was all feeling. Interestingly, my mother was full of male energy, or yang, and my father embodied female energy, or yin.

I believe at one point in our evolutionary history we humans had better balance between yin and yang. The older I get, and the more I go within myself, the more balanced I feel, which may be why I feel such an affinity for that balance in Terry. She is a female dog, so she is allowing, passive, understanding, and spiritually attuned. At the same time, she is also protective and linear. But her female aspects allow her to hold contradictory points of view without becoming confused.

When I examine the unconditional love I feel for Terry, there is one thing about this relationship that causes me grief: I don't know what I will do when Terry passes over. I never felt this way with my mother, my father, or my friends. When they died, I knew they were on a journey to a higher level of understanding. Terry *already* understands, so when she goes I know I will feel that some part of me will have gone with her. It will be difficult to live without Terry's constant reminders that I am capable of unconditional love. I will miss her unconditional love, but not as much as I will miss mine.

As time passes I'm forced to confront the prospect of Terry's death, and to reexamine what I know about death itself. Intellectually I realize that what we perceive as death is just a change of form. But because I'm physical, I will miss Terry deeply. Sometimes I think I'll get another dog right away. Even now, while Terry is still in my life, I find myself wanting to surround myself with animals. I want birds in the house, and I want a cat; because of Terry, I would be happy living with a menagerie. It's wonderful to relate to living things that don't speak, that don't judge, and don't blame. They are always an instant removed from timelessness. They point the way to a state of being we humans can only aspire to.

Terry

Since my MM is my child I hope I can teach her that grow-ing up is essential to aging well. And the older she gets the further inside herself she should look. The more deeply she learns to love, the younger she'll be when she dies.

Shirley

I read somewhere that where there is no resistance there is no harm. On this Easter weekend more than two thousand years ago, Jesus said if I defend myself, I am attacked. What does that mean? Is having defenses really folly? I once asked the Dalai Lama who his greatest spiritual teacher was, and he said Mao Zedong—leader of the nation that invaded Tibet, forcing the Dalai Lama into exile and torturing and killing many Tibetan Buddhist monks. Too many of us see other people as potential threats, instead of teachers. All of our structures and our laws, our codes, our morality and our legal definitions, our penalties, our armaments, even our ethics are based on an eye for an eye, a tooth for a tooth. I think we don't understand that these are Karmic concepts. The laws of Karma are perfect: if we hurt another that hurt will return to us. Energy always returns to the source. Each time we defend ourselves we've made the fear real, and our terror justified. It's a terrible catch-22. Is that what Jesus meant when he said turn the other cheek and if you are hit, turn it again? He might have been crucified, but he didn't die.

Years ago, on a trip home from India I happened to be seated next to the former Prime Minister of India, Jawaharlal Nehru. As we peered out the airplane window at the concrete towers of Manhattan, he told me the city below him looked overwhelming. "I could find that frightening," he said. "But instead I imagine that I am standing in the doorway of the hut in India where I lived as a child; the doors are flung open, allowing the winds of change to blow about my feet, but not to knock me over." After we landed, I went to swat an insect that somehow had gotten into the cabin, and he said, "Don't kill that gnat, you don't know what or who it might have been."

Does the transmigration of souls mean we all spend lifetimes as animals? Will we possibly be animals again? If so, we should certainly take a closer look at how we treat them.

Is it true that when we are born into a human body that it is perfect and capable of immortality if the mind does not abuse it?

Let's say for a moment that sickness is a decision made by the mind. If this is so, we are not the *victims* of illness, but its *perpetrators*. Like a blockage in our veins that keeps blood from circulating through the heart, sickness is a barrier we create against God, peace, and the energy of the natural world, perhaps to learn how much power we have. Sickness is self-deception because we've succumbed to the delusion that what God created—the body and even consciousness itself—is not perfect and whole. But for some of us, sickness is the only time we allow ourselves to slow down, the only excuse we'll accept for extricating ourselves from the overwhelming pressures of everyday life.

Sickness is not only a defense against God's perfection, but also against the solace of friends and family. We go to extraordinary lengths to prove the lie that we are not meant to be happy, that we are sinful and estranged from God. Even if we accept that sickness is just another reality we create, it's still easy to fall into the trap of thinking that this reality too, is beyond our control. A wise person once said to me that we would do anything to erect sandbags against the tide of happiness rising around us. Sometimes it takes a new life, like Terry, or another person, to help us drag the sandbags down, to help us surrender to the tidal wave of happiness.

I wonder how animals respond to human sicknesses. Do our pets take on some of the burden we place on ourselves with our own minds? I have some arthritis in my right knee, and lately it has been giving me some trouble. When I first noticed this, Sheba began to limp on her right side. Are animals trying to help absolve us of our limitations? And if our dogs live seven to every one of our years, are they dying more quickly because they take on our beliefs that the body is imperfect? Could animals live forever as our companions if we also thought *we* could?

What would it be like if we believed that everything is planned by God for our happiness? If so, would sorrow, pain, and tragedy really be necessary? If we believed in our plan of happiness I think we'd have a happier world. We're taught that Easter is a time for resurrection and salvation. Well, perhaps it's time to rise again, and shed our old beliefs. Perhaps when Jesus said, "Forgive them, for they know not what they do," he meant, "Forgive them, for they know not what they do to themselves." Wouldn't we be reborn if we listened to the God within us? Wouldn't that be our salvation?

I'm trying to learn not to plan; I'm trying to learn just to let it happen. I'm trying not to have a schedule for the next day. In these ways I'm experimenting with taking my guidance from God. I'm going to ask God to resolve my travel plans to Ireland.

Terry

On this Easter weekend I want MM to realize that she can be reborn every moment. The body is perfectly prepared to respond to that idea. But she has to mean it in her soul. When she really means it her world will be filled with Easter light.

When MM is worried it's because she is "conflicted." Sometimes I'm a mirror for her when she's conflicted. At those times she looks at me huddled in my little corner and I think she realizes I'm reflecting her mood because I want her to see what it looks like. It's not a pretty sight. Maybe I'll run over and jump into her lap. Then she will pet me and maybe she'll understand.

Shirley

Because I'm so interested in the mind-body-soul connection, I decided to explore psychic surgery for the arthritis in my joints. I was fascinated by the whole process, and assisted several psychic surgeons in Brazil and the Philippines. When I first asked my psychic surgeon in Brazil how it worked, he said, "The body is only an illusion. My real work is on the aura, on the electromagnetic frequency of the body, not on the flesh. But for you to understand, to believe the healing, I have to give you the illusion of my hands entering your body. But in fact, there is no penetration of the flesh at all, because the flesh is not real. You just believe it is."

Time and again I saw that patients would not believe they were healed unless the body was invaded.

The doctors not only cured the sickness by working on the body's aura, but also by reinforcing the counter-dream of healing the body. I saw psychic healers remove eyes and cleanse the disease behind them. I saw them take out hearts to repair valves. The body was an illusion, but the healing had to be physical for the patient's mind to believe it.

When I assisted in these surgeries, I knelt beside patients from many countries whose languages I did not speak, but during the procedure we could communicate. As witness to their healing I felt the melding of my spirit with theirs. What I saw strengthened my conviction that we are perfect in the first place—and in the second, and in the third.

Terry

Sickness is separation from God and healing is the other dream, the one that delivers us back to God. When MM thinks about leaving the steady joy she feels with me, even if only temporarily, for that movie in Ireland, she feels the sharp edges of sickness coming on. Sickness is a kind of lie. We natural beings may take on the sickness of our human companions, but we know why we do it. We love them.

We do not lie about love. We don't pretend to be happy when we're not. We don't pretend anything. We are capable of shrewdness, but not deceit. I can be manipulative to get what I want, but I can't lie about anything. When we're hurt, we show it. When we're joyful, we show that too. A lot of what we display depends on our human companions.

Shirley

It's Easter morning, and Terry is in my arms. I tell myself I should get up and be productive, but here she is, sleeping with her little face next to mine. Her body is stretched out next to me so I can feel her breathing. She begins to twitch. Is she reflecting the dream I just had of being trampled by huge horses? Their hooves came down on me again and again, yet I was still alive. I take Terry in my arms, her body now jerking violently. Is she having my dream or am I having hers? She wakens, and then places her head under my chin. She lies back, almost in a back-bend with her little feet up in the air, completely unself-conscious, at one with herself, with me, and with the new Easter day outside. Birdsong begins to filter in through the window, along with a pervasive feeling of all-oneness.

I lie here with Terry, ruminating. Should I have had more children? Should I have adopted the children I wanted to when I was younger? Is that the impulse Terry is bringing out in me? Or is she bringing out a desire to adopt children now? I imagine what this morning would be like with a houseful of children. No, I'm too old to adopt children now. I've earned this peace and quiet. When I was younger, raising my daughter, my child-rearing friends and I got so bogged down in the details of life that a moment like this, lying with a dog in my arms on an Easter morning, feeling that everything is, as my mother would say, one with God, would not have been possible.

I wonder whether mothers who adopt feel that their new baby was meant for them rather than the birth mother. I think so. Certainly, when we adopt animals, they are meant to be with us. I have adopted Terry instead of a child. I've also adopted the other dogs on the ranch. Sheba was the first one that I saved from her fate at the pound. Then I adopted the rest. They all know it, just as they know that Terry is royalty with Egyptian blood, who is here for unearthly reasons.

I am the wind in the weeping willow by the waterfall. I am the dust blowing in from Colorado. I am the fly buzzing against the screen. Terry and I are having this life dream together. Birds chirp, the wind wafts, trees rustle, the flowers smell, dogs bark, the clouds roll by, and Terry and I are in such bliss that nothing would be worth ending this until it ends itself. Finally we get up from reality into the dream we say is real. We both stretch and rise out of bed.

Now I feel hunger. Now I need to go to the bathroom. Now I feel pain in my back. I start thinking: I need to eat and take my vitamins; I must return phone calls, and wish others Happy Easter; I have to make the most of this day. Then I regain my sanity, and remind myself that I know a happier way to live.

Is this what happens when you get older, when you've done most everything, when you've had the experience of being the belle of the ball and you discover that doesn't provide happiness? Overachievement makes me realize I really don't have to achieve anything at all. Am I becoming a happy, peaceful recluse? Do I not like leaving my ranch because the pace of life outside perturbs me? I look out at a faraway hill and it reminds me of the light from within my mountain that played games with me as I sat bug-eyed. It happened at midnight, when I was out walking with a married couple who are close friends. We all saw a luminescence coming from within Sierra Madre. It moved and danced before our eyes as though a spotlight from within the earth was directed at us. We watched for hours, wondering what it wanted us to know. I thought of my mother's vision of lights within the earth.

Dr. John Mack of Harvard once interviewed a man claiming to have been abducted by extraterrestrials, who told this captive the tragic history of their planet. One of their gods was an enormous boulder, within which was stored all the ancestral knowledge of that race. Over time the citizens of that planet learned how to make genetic material and decided it was the future, choosing to move away from the wisdom they had gathered and stored in the boulder since the dawn of time. The boulder watched helplessly as the planet's inhabitants became more and more warlike, unable to interfere with the free will of its people. Eventually civil war destroyed the planet, and now, according to the abducted man, its refugees were roaming the universe looking for a new home.

Here on the ranch I know I am surrounded by eons of vast knowledge. From mountains to pebbles, from trees to shrubs, everything has a conscious and probably cosmic energy. Nothing stays the same, not even the past; everything we see is altered by the way we see it. Even history, because it snakes back to the present, keeps growing and changing. And what about God? Is God different now than He/She was at the beginning?

If God is perfect and all creations complete, then there's nothing to do but let God's plan unfold. If I am peaceful, the world will be. Whenever I feel anxiety about what to do next, I open the sliding door, let Terry out, call the other dogs, and push myself out of the house into the air, sunshine, and sun-bleached colors of the arroyo. Soon the inner turmoil quiets down, and I feel myself beginning to take guidance from above, a most miraculous frame of mind. On this Easter weekend, when others remember sin and redemption, I turn to the wisdom of nature in search of peace.

As we walk away from the ranch house I check the water storage tank. In the Southwest water is gold. Here in New Mexico a drought has been in effect for several years, causing a bark beetle infestation in the pine trees by compromising their immune systems. Even though I have a productive well I'm considering also installing a rain-catching system from my roof. I think of the stream of snowmelt that runs down from the mountains, and I wonder how long it will last.

Cottonwoods sparkle in the light of the sun and I marvel at these trees that guzzle water from the ground yet exude it right back into the world around them. A sharp wind comes up, blowing my hat off, its string under my chin nearly ripping my earrings from my pierced ears. I hear there's a tornado blowing in the eastern part of the state, which is uncommon in New Mexico, and again I wonder what nature is trying to tell us.

Sunlight flashes against the crystals littered across my land. Everywhere I look I see white and pink quartz crystals, as though a volcano of diamonds erupted hundreds of thousands of years ago, scattering its glittering treasure over the landscape. Could that have been the light I thought I saw within the mountain? No, I'm looking for Earth logic when a deeper logic drives a technology not yet understood by us.

Rising above us is my Sierra Madre. They say that because Madre is a female mountain no man must ever climb it without a woman by his side. It is also said that this mountain serves as a magnetic homing device for UFOs. Perhaps that's why there are so many petroglyphs on this land. Usually they depict five concentric circles, which, according to the Hopi, means that in the future we will be going into the fifth world where we will be able to live among all five dimensions.

The dogs scamper ahead and I trudge up to what I've named Crystal Picnic Hill, a relatively high point on the property. My body has a history, as it did on the

Camino in Spain. As we climb, my feet have memory, my ankles have memory, my lower back has memory, and I feel as if I'm trekking back in time. I glimpse kaleidoscopic shards of the past—of ancient civilizations and wars fought with laser light. I see earthquakes and inundation from roiling seas. I see magnificent buildings destroyed and crystal pyramids floating on rainbow clouds of light. Hovercraft take off and land, teachers address throngs eager to learn, and multidimensional beings are worshiped in gleaming sanctuaries. Everything around me comes alive, as though animated by strange unearthly harmonies, echoes of a language from long ago. Colors accompany the tones, all vibrating and throbbing in melodious synchrony that will take on the shapes and forms of future life on earth.

I stand still, awed by these precognitive memories. Will I be a mysterious memory for someone standing on this hill one million years from now? And in my future form will I recognize that newcomer as myself?

Terry jumps up on my leg, bringing me back to

the present. She stops, looks, and waits, as if to make sure that I stay in the here and now. I wonder what I might have experienced on the Camino if I had had her with me. Would she have pacified the wild dogs?

I walk farther on, bringing to mind what happened more recently on this land. Here Kit Carson raided Native American villages prosperous from a vigorous trade in beads, animal skins, and horns. I often wonder what I should do with this land, and I'm waiting for it to tell me. Should it be home to a new community? Will it be the site of a spiritual school taught by beings from the stars, who once again will teach us who we really are? Did we come from the outer reaches of space to save this planet, only to go astray? Perhaps whatever is coming is truly a prelude to what the prophecies and the Bible say will be a thousand years of light. In all this speculation I only know one thing. I will be here. Perhaps Terry will too. I hope so.

I walk on, aware that I am not the only one who feels the magic of this land. Friends and visitors have reported visions of cities floating in the clouds, and encounters with strange, unearthly people. All agree that this land, marked by crystals, will play a prominent role in the planet's future.

Daisy, the most motherly of the dogs, looks back to see if Terry and I are all right. Mountain lions live here, and coyotes, but since there is a human in our pack they won't bother us. I feel safe until I see Spooky off in the distance. He's too far ahead, and I start to worry, but I follow until we're walking high on the northern part of the property. This is alpine country. I see what two years of drought have done to the ponderosa pines. They are dying from the bark beetle and lack of rainfall. What have we done to nature that she doesn't nourish our trees anymore? What will happen to our source of oxygen if the lungs of the planet die?

Where is Terry? I turn around and see her scampering toward me. The other dogs follow. As if hearing a signal of some kind, Spooky dashes up the side of Sierra Madre and disappears into a cave. I remember seeing him shadowbox with coyotes at midnight under the full moon. He enticed the coyotes out of their lairs, and one by one they engaged in mock combat, etched in moonlight, not knowing I was watching the call of the wild.

Our pack waits until Spooky returns to his family of females. He then leads our expedition farther up the slope, stopping to smell elk droppings, bear scat, and other spoor that only the dogs can identify. Sometimes they eat what they find, and sometimes they just sniff and move on. I wonder what exactly determines the outcome. Terry partakes in none of this. She has fresh meat waiting in her palace ranch home.

We walk for hours. At 8,500 feet I feel my breath coming faster. This is a great place to exercise, because at sea level stamina becomes a cinch. I can see Pikes Peak in Colorado to the north and the lights of Santa Fe to the south.

Up ahead an elegant elk drinks from a mountain stream. He turns and gazes into my eyes as I walk toward him. He is unafraid, and has such a commanding, peaceful presence that I feel I have looked into the face of

God. Terry stops, mesmerized. At my command the pack moves on, leaving the elk to his dignity.

Bears are too shy to show themselves, but I can see the dogs catch their scent.

Traces of snow linger in the spring sunlight, sparkling under the shade of the tall pines. Terry bounds ahead, kicking up snow flurries and twirling in the air. She charges at fallen pinecones, then stops and gazes at the endless spectacle of ancient, timeless beauty. I take her often to this high country on my electric golf cart. She sits beside me with her ears flattened against the wind. Sometimes I drive too close to a tree, inspiring her to lunge at its branches. Sometimes in her exuberance she leaps off the cart, and like an athlete she rolls over and over to break her fall.

A light spring snow begins to fill the sky. The dogs slow, and I imagine it is due to their delight at the gentle snowflakes. I hear snowbirds fluttering through the pines. I am awed by the show nature puts on, and am reminded once again how discerning the ancient Indians were to make this paradise their home. The snow subsides as quickly as it came. Terry shakes herself and waits for direction from me.

Whenever I am around gently falling snow I always think about love. When we love a person we dare to risk. We risk losing control of ourselves on one hand, yet on the other we dare to create a new identity, melding our spirit with that of someone else. Are we each, in truth, separate from each other as we pursue our desires and creative expression in life, or are we bound by some unknown agreement that we need each other to learn about ourselves?

I know now that the purpose of being alive is to be known to myself. Without that knowledge my life would be deeply damaged by what I see around me in the "civilized" world. Every dying person I've ever been around has told me that the only thing that matters in life is love. Do I have to die to fully understand that?

Sometimes I've had to grapple with a sad guilt when I moved on from someone in my life who I thought couldn't keep up. Getting to that point was even worse—it was a terrible feeling to try to cope with nourishing my own progress and growth while still preserving the love. I couldn't understand then that moving on enabled each of us to grow at our own pace.

With my human love relationships there were always extenuating circumstances involving work, logistics, creativity, and commitment based on expectations and promises. With love these problems always arose. So when one dares to love another it involves terrible, beautiful risk. Do we humans love while sacrificing ourselves to preserve it? Or must we love and trust that love will endure regardless of proximity?

I realize now that true love for me will be my connection to the Divine. That is the infinite love without worry, and the love that will last regardless of circumstances. Anything less is an illusion. All these years I have been incessantly questioning creation, and now I want to live within it.

As the snow swiftly melts around me I hope that the love I feel all around me today doesn't meet the same fate.

Terry

The answers that MM seeks are hers to create.

What I have created is this: I am written in MM's heart and always will be. And that's all I have to say about that.

Shirley

I shake myself from my reverie, look below us toward the ranch, and decide to go home—home to a new under-standing and hopefully home to a newly created world inside myself. The dogs feel my desire to trek back. They turn, and Spooky bolts out ahead of the pack.

I shout to Sheba to tell Spooky not to go so fast and she runs ahead to deliver the message with that awkward hitch in her stride. Terry gets a cactus needle stuck in her paw and limps over. She won't let me pull it out, though. She does that with her own teeth.

I'm feeling a sharp pain in my foot too, so I find a nice flat rock and take off my shoe and sock to inspect the blister. At the sight I flash back to all those years of dancing, of bloody feet in the dressing room. Terry slips under my leg and gives the blister a lick.

Now that we've stopped walking for a moment I look at my watch and realize we've been out for five hours. I take a sip of precious water. I hope I've brought enough. In all my years of walking and hiking I am reminded again that to be happy and comfortable doesn't take much: a good hat, a good pair of shoes, and water. Anything else is luxury! As I slip my walking shoes back on I wish my privileged Western feet were calloused enough to let me walk barefoot, like the Native American trailblazers who ran across these hills, skimming over rocks, underbrush, cactus, and shards of crystal from another time.

We're moving again, and as we reach an opening in the trees there's Sierra Madre Mountain in the distance, where the lights in the sky go home. I use that mountain as my guide, and orient myself. We walk back through Copper Canyon, which I named for its shimmering metallic earth, studded with emerald trees, piñon bushes, and fragrant juniper. Its cliffs look like they were chiseled by a divine hand. Desert flowers, dandelions, violets, and chamiso blossoms fall like gemstones from God's fingers.

Terry seems to stop for every buttercup. Do they speak a special language to each other? She sniffs and nudges and nibbles until the flower gives itself up to her curiosity.

There's electricity in the air; a lightning storm may be brewing. In the strange greenish light I can't tell the difference between fallen branches and whitened antlers from animals long departed from this world. Sometimes the pack stops as one, alert to some ripple in the consciousness of this land. I don't hear anything, but I feel it.

As our little band gets closer to home, I realize the older dogs have a focus. They want water and something to eat. I see a dust storm in Colorado that likely began on another continent, transported here courtesy of the jet stream. A butterfly blinks and the rest of the cosmos feels the impact.

I remember a time I took a delegation to China and the dust storms off the Mongolian desert blew into Beijing and Shanghai. Everyone got pneumonia but me, although I experienced a permanent change in my endocrine system. East dust met West dust and changed my body forever.

Our pace picks up as the descent becomes less steep. I come to my spiral labyrinth at the top of the mesa closest to the ranch house. Here, as a gift to me, a friend of mine arranged stones in spirals that reflect the movement of human consciousness. I walk here several times a week to resolve whatever is bothering me. Terry scampers around in the labyrinth, knowing this is a sacred place but unable to keep from playing. The other dogs slow down, but stay ahead, knowing the ranch is near. I see the bench I built for meditation, and two trees nearby with smooth stones under them to sit on, and I'm glad to rest a little. Terry sits down and seems to meditate herself. Then, standing on the heart-shaped stone that marks both the entrance and the exit of the labyrinth, I pray for inner peace. I sigh deeply and remember that God is in the air we breathe. When I move again, Terry chases my shadow.

I look back at the snow-capped mountain and the canyon where we have just walked for hours. Is that gray mist rain? I turn to Sierra Madre looming to the east, where sunrise backlights the great mountain every morning. To the west, Perdenal Mountain, sacred to Native Americans, stands majestically with its flat top. I thank all that surrounds me.

As we descend the hill from the labyrinth, I see that Sheba, Sandy, Spooky, and Daisy have disappeared. I know they've gone to the pond to drink and cool off. Terry doesn't join them. She wants me to bathe her in the sink of her palace home. I am her servant. Around a bend in the trail I see the other dogs are up to their necks in the pond, splashing around and gulping the cool water. They emerge and shake themselves, flinging rainbow drops into the waning sunlight. Terry stands regally and holds her head high with one paw poised in the air, waiting for their foolishness to cease before she leads me to our ranch house.

In the distance I see another dog, a dog I've never seen before, standing in my garden. Spooky spots it too, and charges down the path, followed closely by the three females, with Terry bringing up the rear. When they reach New Dog, there is no growling or snarling. The pack just forms a circle. Terry returns to me. I fear for the New Dog, and call off the females. They obey. Spooky and New Dog silently confront each other. Neither moves. I know now that New Dog is male. Time stands still. Will it be peace or war? Then Terry breaks away from me and slowly approaches the standoff. I wait with the other females, my heart pounding, knowing I shouldn't interfere. Could New Dog be another Spirit Dog bringing us his own stories from other places and other times?

Terry slowly positions herself between the two males. She looks toward Spooky. His ears lie back against his head, deferring to her. She turns toward New Dog. He does nothing. She then saunters toward him, stops, and seductively rolls over on her back. New Dog is nonplussed. He turns, spots a bush, lifts his leg, and pees. Spooky stands stock-still. Then he saunters over to the bush, lifts his leg and pees on it too. Terry then moves to the bush, lifts *her* leg, and then *she* pees on it! Then she calmly moves away. Spooky sits by the bush and waits. After a long few moments, New Dog simply strolls off into the hills. I watch until he disappears into the deepening twilight, then Terry and I head into the house.

Suddenly, and shockingly loud, the telephone rings. With some trepidation I answer. It is the producer from Northern Ireland. "I'm sorry to tell you this," he says, "but the money fell through. So I guess you won't be coming to our fair land."

After some inanely comforting conversation, I hang up and shriek with happiness. Terry jumps into my arms and kisses my cheek. Has she really understood what just happened?

She bounds around with her twinkling butt and sparkling feet. She finds a toy and tosses it into the air for me to catch. Then she walks straight to the sink for me to wash the dirt off her feet. After her bath, I give her a little bone and she twirls three times: one for mind, one for body, and one for spirit. Then Terry curls up in her little bed and goes right to sleep, as if to say, I knew it all along.

I walk outside, disrobe, and climb into the hot tub. Daisy sits beside it, dozing in the evening sun. Sheba looks out over the mountains. Sandy is nowhere to be seen, but I spot Spooky slipping like a silent wraith around the corner of the house.

I sigh deeply as I realize that in a few days it will be my birthday.

"What a gift life is," I think. "Everything happens just as it should. And I am blessed with the luck of the Irish."

Then I remember something Terry said to me once. "Give me a bone and I'll be happy . . . give me a home in your heart and *you* will."